THE HANDBOOK O
PURCHASING

From boycotts of plastics and palm oil by consumers, to the tracking of carbon footprints and modern slavery in their supply chains by businesses, buying ethically has now fully captured the public interest. *The Handbook of Ethical Purchasing* is designed to help both ordinary people and industry professionals to understand this new movement, its political background and, most importantly, how to become involved more effectively.

By looking in turn at sustainable supply chain management by companies, green public procurement by governments, and the ethical choices made by consumers, this book operates as a practical handbook for people across all industries and sectors to become involved in the important changes that need to be made. It provides the key principles, language, and techniques that companies, campaigners, certification schemes, and regulators are beginning to use to address the moral, practical, and political problems that commonly occur in this transition to more ethical economies.

Written by a leading authority on ethical consumption, Rob Harrison, the book provides the reader with the tools to operate with confidence and effectiveness in an easy-to-access format. It also provides a useful structure to understand this new subject area for students of marketing, supply chain management, and business studies generally.

Rob Harrison is one of three founder members of the Ethical Consumer Research Association in the UK. He has been an editor and writer at *Ethical Consumer Magazine* since that time and has spoken widely in the press, on radio, and on TV, as well as to universities and campaign groups around the world, on the importance of facilitating ethical consumption in a globalised marketplace. He has also acted as a consultant to NGOs, businesses, governments, and consumers' associations around the world on how to make markets work for social change.

THE HANDBOOK OF ETHICAL PURCHASING

Principles and Practice

Rob Harrison

Routledge
Taylor & Francis Group

LONDON AND NEW YORK

First published 2022
by Routledge
2 Park Square, Milton Park, Abingdon, Oxon OX14 4RN

and by Routledge
605 Third Avenue, New York, NY 10158

Routledge is an imprint of the Taylor & Francis Group, an informa business

© 2022 Rob Harrison

British Library Cataloguing-in-Publication Data
A catalogue record for this book is available from the British Library

Library of Congress Cataloging-in-Publication Data
Names: Harrison, Rob, 1961- author.
Title: The handbook of ethical purchasing : principles and practice / Rob Harrison.
Description: Abingdon, Oxon ; New York, NY : Routledge, 2022. | Includes bibliographical references and index.
Identifiers: LCCN 2021017555 (print) | LCCN 2021017556 (ebook) | ISBN 9781032059945 (hardback) | ISBN 9781032059952 (paperback) | ISBN 9781003200185 (ebook)
Subjects: LCSH: Purchasing—Moral and ethical aspects. | Consumption (Economics)—Moral and ethical aspects.
Classification: LCC HF5437 .H325 2022 (print) | LCC HF5437 (ebook) | DDC 178—dcundefined
LC record available at https://lccn.loc.gov/2021017555
LC ebook record available at https://lccn.loc.gov/2021017556

ISBN: 978-1-032-05994-5 (hbk)
ISBN: 978-1-032-05995-2 (pbk)
ISBN: 978-1-003-20018-5 (ebk)

DOI: 10.4324/9781003200185

Typeset in Joanna
by codeMantra

CONTENTS

PREFACE

As this book goes on to explain, ethical purchasing activities began to appear spontaneously, everywhere, at the end of the 20th century to address both general injustices and oppression (like the boycott of apartheid South Africa) as well as specific problems thrown up by the unregulated globalisation of markets (like factory conditions in the clothing industry).

Nowadays, whole institutions and bureaucracies have grown up to manage, refine, and respond to the many hundreds of campaigns and interventions that now occur annually. In addition, new companies are forming daily to bring new 'ethical' products to markets everywhere.

In my day job, at Ethical Consumer Research Association, I have been lucky enough, over the years, to work with all these types of institutions, from governments to companies and from campaigners to consumer groups. As this movement grows, I have seen more and more people beginning to work in areas which are touched by it, but who struggle at least initially to understand some of its key motivations and dynamics.

This book therefore began life as a project called 'Principles of Ethical Purchasing'. The idea was that reading about ethical purchasing as a series of principles might be a useful way of learning about it for people coming completely new to the subject   as well as for more seasoned participants who might not know the full scope and extent of what was happening elsewhere. There was even an aspiration that it could become a text for the kind of formal educational programmes which the principles themselves argue is needed.

As you will have noticed, the book is broken down into a series of chapters which, in the main, look at each of the key institutions in turn. There is also a paragraph numbering system, which is mainly used to help keep track of all these cross-cutting principles, ideas, and themes. It will be useful for those who want to dip into the book to read the chapter for the institution they are working in to see the important links to other areas, and avoids too much repetition for people who want to read the whole thing.

For those who do want to read from Chapters 1 to 10, it may be worth knowing that it has been arranged with at least one eye on the historical order of events in the movement's growth.

Next, there are two apologies to make. First, expressions such as 'ethical product' or 'ethical market' appear throughout this book. Of course, this is technically a nonsense, because a product cannot, of itself, have moral decision-making capacity. Nevertheless, this approach is in common usage, everyone knows what it means, and it is cumbersome to write it out properly each time as, for example, 'a product created or sold with certain ethical attributes'.

Second, although a generalist book does have advantages, such as noticing trends and links that apply across many specialist areas, it will almost certainly not be as learned within each specialist area like procurement, economics, or sociology as those written by specialists themselves. The 'references and notes' sections at the end of each chapter should of course provide links to these more specialist texts for those that want them. But if you do find elements which you think need particular attention, do let me know. It is a fast-moving field, and corrections or improvements for any future editions that may arise are welcome. I can usually be contacted via the Ethical Consumer research hub.

Penultimately, some thanks are appropriate. This work would not have been possible without the contributions of the many thousands of people who have supported the Ethical Consumer Research Association over its more than 30 years of life. This includes, but is not limited to, subscribers to the magazine, colleagues, research partners, and social investors.

And finally a call to action. Almost everyone I meet working in this area is motivated to do so because they want to help address inequalities and other damaging impacts thrown up by the economic systems we are operating within. As the ethical purchasing movement becomes more bureaucratic and technical, it can become easier to lose sight of this. So although this book is primarily a technical handbook with practical ideas and suggestions, I do occasionally let slip just how exasperating I find some current business behaviour and economic discourse around today.

This book's real uniqueness lies in identifying all this activity as a 'movement' and providing a broader understanding about how each element sits within it. It observes how effective ethical purchasing commonly involves complex collective actions across sectors and that to have the most lasting impact it needs all these elements to be working together and for everyone to become involved.

Rob Harrison
March 2021

ABBREVIATIONS

ASDA	Associated Dairies (UK Supermarket group)
BCI	Better Cotton Initiative
BRE	Building Research Establishment
CDP	Carbon Disclosure Project
CFCs	Chlorofluorocarbons
CIPS	Chartered Institute of Purchasing and Supply
CIWF	Compassion in World Farming
CSO	Civil Society Organisation
CSR	Corporate Social Responsibility
DfID	UK Department for International Development
ECRA	Ethical Consumer Research Association
EIA	Environmental Investigation Agency
EICC	Electronic Industry Citizenship Coalition
EPEAT	Electronic Product Environmental Assessment Tool (USA)
ESG	Environmental, Social, and Governance (Investment)
ETAG	Ethical Trading Action Group
ETI	Ethical Trading Initiative
EU	European Union
FLA	Fair Labor Association (USA)
FoE	Friends of the Earth
FSC	Forest Stewardship Council
GATT	General Agreement on Tariffs and Trade

GDP   Gross Domestic Product
GM   Genetically Modified
GOTS   Global Organic Textile Standard
GRI   Global Reporting Initiative
H&M   Hennes & Mauritz (Swedish clothing company)
ICLEI   International Council for Local Environmental Initiatives
ILO   International Labour Organisation
LCA   Life-Cycle Analysis or Life-Cycle Assessment
MNC   Multinational Company/Corporation
MSC   Marine Stewardship Council
MSI   multi-Stakeholder Initiative
NEF   New Economics Foundation
NFU   National Farmers Union
NGO   Non-Governmental Organisation
PEFC   Program for the Endorsement of Forest Certification
RFID   Radio-Frequency Identification
RSPCA   Royal Society for the Prevention of Cruelty to Animals
RSPO   Roundtable on Sustainable Palm Oil
SDGs   Sustainable Development Goals
SEDEX   Supplier Ethical Data Exchange
SGS   Société Générale de Surveillance (Swiss auditor)
SRI   Socially Responsible Investment
UN   United Nations
UTZ   Universal Trade Zone (Dutch ethical label)
WTO   World Trade Organisation
WWF   World Wide Fund for Nature

1

UNDERSTANDING THE BASIC PRINCIPLES

1.1 The language of ethics has evolved to look at good, or right or moral choices

Ethics is a word used to describe that area of human activity whereby moral or good or right choices are discussed. Ethics has a long history of serious study from Greek philosophers such as Aristotle to modern ethicists such as Professor Peter Singer – an Australian proponent of the idea that animals should have rights.

Although it is taught as a subject in many universities, it is not normally covered in schools, and is not therefore a word which many people use with much confidence. This applies equally to teenagers out shopping on Saturday and chief executives of multinational oil companies.

Nevertheless, most people's lives – when examined in detail – contain many discussions and assumptions about ethical or moral choices both within and outside markets. Most people act ethically sometimes without even thinking of it as ethical: when they are kind to neighbours, for example, or when they hold a door open for someone carrying a baby.

DOI: 10.4324/9781003200185-1

The notion of ethics, though, generally focuses on the question of how humans should live together, and therefore concerns itself with ideas of 'civil society' or 'community' or of the 'common good'. Ethical choices are, therefore, normally those that consider the impact of our decisions not only on ourselves but also on other people around us.

1.1.1 It covers both religious and political ideas of what is good

Ethics is a very broad subject area which includes discussion of religious rules, such as you shall not kill, as well as political propositions, such as richer people should pay more tax to help people who don't have enough. Although some political and religious conversations may concern ethics, not all will do. 'Vote for me because I'll make you richer' is not normally seen as an ethical proposition, whereas the statement 'vote for me because I support free universal healthcare' is more likely to be an ethically motivated statement.

1.1.2 What is ethical isn't always agreed by everyone

It is useful to recognise that from a sociological point of view, we can be observed as often having different ethical standpoints. Some people, for example, think that eating animals is wrong, whilst others do not. Some people think that building nuclear weapons is wrong. Other people think that it's a necessary activity in a dangerous world. In most complex societies, we have learned to rub along with people with different ethical standpoints most of the time.

Ethical discussions can also get tricky in the real world because when we think we agree, we might not. Is unethical child labour anyone working under 16 years of age or 15 (as it is in some countries)? Are children working at weekends on family farms OK? If it is safe?

1.1.3 There are some areas however where there is quite a lot of agreement

In most societies, core areas of ethical agreement exist. Killing humans for personal gain, for example, is normally outlawed. In addition, purchasing, because it is commonly concerned with manufactured goods, also tends to have core areas of ethical agreement around manufacturing processes. A majority of people in all societies, for example, agree that factories should not poison local rivers with effluent or employ children on a full-time basis. The notion of 'socially responsible business behaviour' has emerged in this space to try to specifically understand some elements of business ethics. Many companies have claimed to be socially responsible when it is obvious to most people that they are not. This has not helped the credibility of the idea of socially responsible business much, and we cover this and the idea of greenwash in more detail in Section 2.3.1 and elsewhere.

Some philosophers have suggested that globalisation has brought with it some emerging global ethical values. The UN's 17 Sustainable Development Goals – which include eradicating hunger and providing universal primary education – are an example of this kind of emergence. These appear with some other broad ethical frameworks in Appendix 1.

We also look at other general principles such as 'do no harm' in Section 7.1.3 and elsewhere.

1.2 Purchasing is a word which can be used for both big and small economic actors

Purchasing is a word used to describe the exchange of money for a product or service. The word purchasing, used in its broadest sense, can cover everything from the buying of a packet of sweets by a child at the corner shop to the 'procurement' of a road-building programme by a government with all its attendant rules and temptations for corruption.

1.2.1 Purchasing is increasing because of economic growth and the current popularity of markets

The encroachment and refinement of market ideas on ever-broader areas of society mean that a wider range of goods and services can be purchased than previously. For example, private home care visits for elderly relatives and a range of on-line educational choices are two of many such recent innovations. Marxists, who tend to quite like long words, call this process commodification.

In addition, economic growth, globalisation of markets, and rising incomes also mean that quantitatively more people are buying many more things than they might have done just 40 years ago. In China, for example, the idea of choice in markets has gone from an unacceptable bourgeoisie fixation to an idealised collective goal.

We also look at the increase in purchasing by multinational corporations across national borders in Chapter 4.

1.3 Ethical purchasing is an observable phenomenon

Whatever we think of it, ethical purchasing is something which we can observe taking place around us in the 21st century. People are buying free-range eggs, Fairtrade coffees and organic juices in the UK, for example. There was a big increase in this type of activity in the last two decades of the 20th century in Western Europe and North America particularly (see Chapter 2).

1.3.1 It can be observed being practised by a wide range of actors

Looking at the wider phenomenon of 'ethical purchasing' allows this book to explain that it is not something that just individuals do. Ethical purchasing can be observed in clubs, societies, businesses, charities, local authorities, governments, and even supranational institutions. Some of the complex internal developments within institutions around ethical purchasing are discussed in more detail in Chapters 4–6 and demonstrate how collective this kind of activity can be.

This book is designed to act as a useful guide to available principles for all types of economic actor.

1.3.2 In can be observed happening all around the world

For an ethical purchase to take place, all that is required is choice (more than one product to choose from) and information about ethical impacts. There are few countries which do not have these elements in at least some markets. Although the UK has probably some of the most developed 'ethical markets', ethical purchase activity has been identified in Hungary, Chile, Japan, Australia, South Africa, Canada, India, Brazil, the USA, and China, to name but ten.

1.3.3 Ethical purchasers are looking at ethics in addition to price and quality

One of the most common misunderstandings about ethical purchasing is that ethics is the primary concern when this kind of purchasing takes place.

Although this is the case in some circumstances, in the majority of cases ethics is a third factor once information on price (what is affordable) and quality (what works) has been weighed up. This has led some misguided manufacturers to produce either very expensive ethical products or less effective ethical products, and then wonder why they are not very successful (see Section 9.3).

1.3.4 On occasions ethics has grown to become an important concern for the majority of purchasers in a market

Although at first ethical buying behaviours were marginal, they are fast becoming a mainstream concern in many markets. Buying ethically is now recognised as one of the most frequently practised political activities across Europe (after voting and petitions), and in some specific cases as many as 75% of people have become involved (Figure 1.1).

The table below uses data amalgamated from more than 100 opinion surveys from consumers around the world which ask them about their ethical buying habits. This pattern, showing a small core of activists but a majority of people occasionally active, is repeated in most countries in the world, including emerging economies such as Brazil, China, and India.

And although there are problems with the accuracy of surveys generally, in 'mature ethical markets' which have been around for more than ten years, we can see ethical products sometimes growing to take a majority market share. The examples most commonly used are Fairtrade bananas in Switzerland (56% of the market) and tea brands in the UK (more than 80% of sales labelled 'ethical' in some way). It is no longer ridiculous to suggest that in the future, most consumer markets could look something like this.

It is possible that a spectrum of this kind – with a few very ethical and a majority sometimes ethical – might also look similar if applied to companies or other institutions discussed in this book.

Always ethical	Sometimes ethical	Can't be bothered
5-10%	60-75%	20-30%

Figure 1.1 Consolidated survey data on consumer ethical buying intentions 1989–2018.

1.3.5 Sometimes ethical purchasing may be given different names like sustainable procurement or green shopping

Although many thousands of people now talk about ethical purchasing on a daily basis, they may use different names for it. We come across all these terms in later chapters of this book and they include political consumption (10.5.4), green procurement (4.3, 6.4), and sustainable supply chain management (4.3.1). I have chosen to use the term ethical purchasing here because it appears to cast the net most broadly. 'Green' sometimes just means environmental and may not look at social issues. Sustainable usually embraces both environmental and social issues these days, but rarely covers animal welfare or animal rights concerns. 'Ethical' can not only draw in all these areas but can also include ideas of socially responsible approaches to more financial matters like pricing, marketing, remuneration, tax payment, and political lobbying.

Section 10.5.2 discusses how language in this field is developing more generally.

1.3.6 By identifying ethical purchasing as a single phenomenon, it is possible to both study it and advocate for its wider encouragement

The purpose of this book is to describe the phenomenon of ethical purchasing and in doing so, to draw boundaries around it. Whilst there are many books on fair trade or boycotts or sustainable procurement by governments, these rarely try to situate them within what might be seen as a broader movement for economic change. It is in identifying this broader movement that the main usefulness of the idea of ethical purchasing is found.

First, it is a useful idea because the different elements can be studied together. This means that learning from one area can be carried across to another. For example, campaigners can learn that researching and publishing regular rankings of the performance of consumer brands against a certain ethical issue is a good way of driving change because it simultaneously shames the worst performers while congratulating the best (see Section 3.5).

Second, it is useful because this makes it possible to advocate its wider encouragement. This takes place throughout this book. The idea that it can self-consciously become a movement and thereby gain greater impetus is also discussed at the end of this book in Theoretical Principles (Chapter

10). Also covered there is the idea that ethical purchasing is part of an even broader movement seeking ethics across all economic transactions (see 10.3).

1.4 Ethical purchasing is increasing in the 21st century

1.4.1 It is increasing because markets are not very good at ethics

Global markets may have done well at delivering a wide range of innovative products and apparently low prices, but they have failed to do this in a way which has not caused unacceptable levels of environmental damage, increased pressure on human rights, and caused widespread problems for other species. This is explored in more detail in Chapter 10 (Theoretical Principles) which goes further by suggesting that failure to deal with 'externalities' in global markets is creating an existential threat for humanity. It also notes how campaigners are using 'race-to-the-bottom' as an expression to describe how some unregulated markets are currently operating to reward the least ethical companies and punish the best.

In addition, the dominant organisational and management language (economics) has not yet shown an ability to even discuss ethical issues in a particularly coherent way, and sometimes shows open hostility to discussion of ethics within it (see 10.8).

1.4.2 It is increasing because of globalisation and 'regulatory capture'

It is widely agreed that it is far better if markets are made to behave ethically because governments regulate or ban unacceptable activities. Children under the age of 10 were, for example, prohibited from working in factories in the UK by the Factory Acts of the 1840s. Two factors made this kind of intervention more difficult in the late 20th century:

(a) Globalisation of production makes regulatory intervention at a national level more difficult (the Dutch government cannot ban child labour in Pakistan for example).

(b) Multinational companies have grown so big as to have, in many instances, 'captured' their regulators, and governments have become afraid of regulating. Multinationals can behave in crass, self-interested ways and may, for example, threaten to 'leave' a country if regulations which harm their financial interests are introduced (see 10.1.4).

1.4.3 It is increasing because it is effective at driving change to some degree

If campaign groups or organisations with a social purpose can see that addressing ethics in markets generally and with purchasers in particular can deliver social and environmental improvements, then it is self-evident that they will copy and try to use similar tactics in future campaigns. This we can observe happening in the sphere of ethical purchasing. The number of people employed in checking ethical behaviour of companies is now in the thousands globally. And campaigns involving both individual consumers (Chapter 2) and organisational purchasers (Chapters 3–6) can clearly demonstrate measurable successes.

Of course, this does not mean that every ethical purchasing campaign is successful. Like any other campaign for political change, they can be badly run, badly promoted, and even ill conceived. The diamond industry's campaign to certify as 'conflict free' its own supply chains is a standard case study, for example, in how not to do it. There are many others.

1.4.4 It is not a substitute for regulation but a useful additional tool

Although regulation can be hard to achieve (see 1.4.2), when properly implemented it can normally change market behaviour more effectively than purchaser action alone. The ban on the sale of high-energy (incandescent) light bulbs in Europe is just one example of many. The preference for regulatory solutions over ethical market campaigns is therefore a running theme throughout this book, although it should be noted that the two are not necessarily mutually exclusive. At Section 3.1.1, for example, we look at how campaigners can use purchasing campaigns to complement working for regulatory changes in situations where industry behaviour is the cause of a problem.

1.5 Ethical purchasing is normally practised to channel economic resources towards more ethical products and suppliers and away from more problematic ones

The mechanism with which ethical buying creates pressure for change is so self-evident that it is practised across cultures and times without much reflection or explanation occurring (see e.g. boycotts and positive buying in Chapter 2). If I have to part with my money, I would rather it went to someone I liked rather than someone I didn't. And ethical behaviour, or the lack of it, is normally one element we use in deciding whether we like someone. This can work on every level from passing by the grumpy stallholder in the market who is mean to his kids, to buying from a global multinational like Patagonia which has convinced us of its desire to behave ethically (see 2.6.1(b)). It is possible to observe change happening in at least five main ways, and these are discussed next. And later on, in Chapter 3, we can see how, in real world campaigns, all these five elements can be at play at the same time.

1.5.1 *Change can occur through growth of ethical markets*

For most economists, and indeed many other people, an ethical position in a market is just another preference like style or colour or flavour. If more people are buying white cars this year, then manufacturers will make more white cars and white paint manufacturers will employ more people. In the same way, therefore, if more people buy organic bread, for example, then more organic bread will be made. This is turn will create more demand for organic flour, which will ultimately increase the area of land farmed under a system which promotes greater biodiversity.

Using this model and the example of organic bread, it is possible to visualise a utopian future where almost all bread producers use organic flour, the countryside is alive with insects and birds, and ethical producers have grown to become the dominant providers in this market. People and organisations, by purchasing ethically, have persuaded producers to change production methods. Bread companies which dislike organic farming have watched their share of the market decline and seen the growth of competitors which have more warmly embraced it. They were forced to choose whether to join in or to shut shop.

To some degree we have been able to observe this happening in some UK markets. The impact of Fairtrade coffee in the UK is just one example (see 3.4.1), and we have already mentioned a couple of others above where 'ethical' products are beginning to take a majority market share.

Of course, the reality is much more complex. Companies seeing a decline in market share, for example, can become involved in trying to undermine ethical standards through setting up competing ethical schemes (8.3.1).

1.5.2 Change can also occur through social pressure

Academic studies of consumer boycotts particularly have noted how some campaigns seek to create change by being 'expressive' rather than 'instrumental'. By this, they mean that moral pressure can create change even when economic pressure is less clearly evidenced. We see in Chapter 2 how boycotts can be an expression of moral opprobrium or outrage and can seek to ostracise or otherwise put pressure on individuals working for companies which are creating problems. The degree to which tobacco and more recently fossil fuels have become tainted business areas to operate in and now have trouble recruiting good staff (see 10.3.3) is just one example. And although 'positive buying' campaigns persuading people to buy ethical products don't seek to work in this way, they can't help but create a comparison with less ethical competitors making the same products.

1.5.3 Change by providing a model for how ethical production can work

In Chapter 3, we see how some campaigners have set up companies or production systems to demonstrate to hostile or unconvinced industries that more ethical modes of production are possible. And in Chapter 4, we explore the idea that civil society campaigning in this space is about creating a moral framework for production in globalised markets where some multinational companies appear to be operating without much evidence of a moral compass (4.2).

1.5.4 Change through creating business champions for social causes

As we have identified above, self-interested lobbying against regulations which threaten corporate profitability is a core problem in the era in which ethical purchasing has emerged. Throughout this book, we can observe how one benefit of market campaigning is that it can either create or support businesses whose interests will coincide with social or environmental interventions. If 'business interests' are not all speaking with one voice, it can give regulators more courage to take them on. The Fair Tax Mark in the UK, for example, has been particularly adept as working with its certified companies to encourage specific government regulations on tax avoidance (see 3.1.1).

1.5.5 Change through building an economy of mission-driven businesses

In Section 10.9, we discuss the observation that the growth of ethical purchasing is also a key factor in the emergence of new mission-oriented company types. For those that have problem with profit-seeking businesses generally, even those producing ethically certified products, another modified vision of the utopian future mentioned above is of one where the majority of producers operate with new mission-driven organisational forms.

1.6 Purchasers have power where there is a choice between producers

1.6.1 Even a choice between two gives leverage

Although some markets still have monopoly providers – railways, utilities, and search engines are three that come to mind – the marketisation of societies mentioned above has meant that, particularly for people living in big cities, a choice of providers is now common. Ordinary economics recognise that this can give economic power to a purchaser, but for purchasers considering ethical or political issues, this can also give them, in some senses, a political power.

In the town where I was growing up in the 1970s, there were two local shops. One was run by a man who put adverts for far-right marches (National Front) in the window of his shop. The other was not. I was not the only person who did not buy from him.

1.6.2 Purchaser power, both ethical and otherwise, is related to the size of the purchase value relative to the size of the supplier

Where the value of the purchase is large (a local authority commissioning a building for example), the power to ask for 'special' requirements is much greater (the employment of local people for example). One of my favourite quotes which illustrate this point comes from a building contractor Michael Conlon working for Preston Council in 2018: "If a client said to me, 'I want all your staff to wear kilts', I'd say: 'Which tartan would you prefer?'"

Whilst some buyers are the only customer of a company and can effectively dictate the conditions of production, in other circumstances – such as an individual buying a pack of coffee from the world's biggest food multinational – that 'power' is tiny. This is why many collective actions have mushroomed in this space in order to aggregate millions of smaller purchasers into an important force (see Chapters 2 and 3).

It is quite evident from studies of consumer boycotts that, on occasion, this aggregated power can be significant. A well-studied case occurred in 1995 when Shell decided to dump an old oil platform by towing it out to sea and sinking it. In what became known as the Bent Spar boycott, as many as 70% of consumers in some parts of Germany stopped using Shell petrol stations as a result of the campaign. One of the biggest multinational companies in the world was forced to capitulate within weeks of the campaign beginning despite its protests that its approach was 'scientifically valid'.

1.6.3 It is a power which has been likened to voting or democratic power

Some people have compared purchasing with voting. In some senses this is useful because purchasing, like voting, is more than mere persuasion or argument. If a majority feels differently to you on an ethical issue and boycotts your products, no matter how wrong you may think they are, you still have to accede to their wishes to keep trading. This was the case with Brent Spar. It also occurred during the Alabama bus boycotts over racially segregated seating rules in the 1960s. In Alabama, some bus company owners inexplicably believed strongly in racial segregation. They held out for nine months and virtual bankruptcy before finally admitting defeat.

In other senses, likening purchasing to voting is problematic because richer people could be seen as having a greater vote. This obviously applies less to bread (which everyone buys in roughly similar quantities) than it does to luxury cars (only bought by the super-rich), but it is one of many reasons to prefer electoral democracy whenever this is possible.

Purchasing also has some advantages over electoral democracy, in that it can be exercised (for some products) every day rather than annually or every four or five years in a normal voting cycle. The contested idea of purchase voting is discussed in more detail under theoretical principles in Section 10.7.

1.6.4 With power comes responsibility

It is widely recognised that power should be exercised with responsibility and it has been expressed in this area by notions such as responsible consumption and socially responsible investment. It is sometimes useful in political campaigns to suggest that consumers or other purchasers are not acting responsibly and may even be profiting from an unethical activity. This occurred, for example, when local authorities and churches were criticised for investing in armaments companies during the Vietnam War.

However, claiming that ordinary consumers are responsible for every detail of hugely complex supply chains (a mobile phone has more than 300 individual components for example) is also recognised as problematic. Regulators and producers must also take responsibility and with their greater access to information about production should potentially bear a greater share of responsibility (see 2.8).

It is also worth noting that one of the UN's 17 Sustainable Developments Goals appearing in Appendix 1 and also mentioned above is 'Responsible Consumption and Production'.

1.6.5 Responsibility to purchase ethically exists at every stage in a supply chain

'Supply chain' is an expression used to describe each step in the often complex process of bringing modern products to markets. Clothing is a well-studied example which commonly starts with a cotton farmer who sells to a trader, who sells to a spinning factory to make yarn, which sells to a cloth-maker to weave and dye, which sells to a cutting and making factory, which sells to a retailing brand like H&M, and finally to the consumer. The retailer might call this a six-stage supply chain.

In the same sense that we have a moral (but not always legal) responsibility to try to rescue a drowning person as we pass by, we should act to prevent harm if we know or should know about it.

A moral obligation to purchase responsibly, therefore, not only exists at each stage in a supply chain, but also falls on regulators to prevent abuse and encourage good practice.

In the 1990s, where 'outsourcing' production to other companies was beginning to catch on both in supply chains and in government, it was not unknown for organisations to try to claim that problems like low pay or child labour further down a supply chain were not their responsibility. Almost no one was convinced by this argument, and a classic case occurred during the boycott of the footwear multinational Nike, which is covered in more detail in Section 3.3.1.

1.7 Working collectively with other purchasers normally creates the greatest impact

We saw in Section 1.5.2 that, self-evidently, the power of purchasers to create more ethical supply chains is related to the size of the purchase value relative to the size of the supplier. Because much of modern global commerce is now dominated by huge global corporations, it can be quite difficult for the ethical concerns of even mid-sized purchasers to be taken seriously, let alone the relatively tiny impact of an individual consumer. And it is for this reason that many thousands of collective actions have sprung up around the globe to try to address ethical issues in markets. We see in Section 2.2.1 how some consumer boycotts became adopted by millions of people in countries around the world and had real impact on global events. We also see how much collective action these days is focussed on putting 'ethically approved' labels on 'good' products or companies. One of the main purposes of this book is to explore this in detail, and it is covered in many other sections but particularly in Chapter 8.

We also learn in Chapter 5 how even big purchasers like local authorities have joined together to share information and ideas around sustainable purchasing.

And we also learn in Section 10.8 how this idea of collective action around ethical issues is a direct challenge to mainstream economic ideas, which argue that markets will function effectively if each purchaser just buys according to their own self-interest.

Finally, it is worth mentioning that surveys tell us that one of the main barriers to individual consumers buying ethically is the belief that their tiny impact will not make a difference. Focussing the conversation on how this movement is really one of collective actions can help to some degree address these fears.

1.8 Communicating ethical purchasing choices is key to effectiveness

As we saw in Section 1.3.3, most ethical purchasers are taking ethics into account in addition to price and quality. This means that sellers don't always know whether their relatively ethical approach is what influenced someone to buy from them, or alternatively that their careless approach to business ethics is what is causing people to avoid them. Buyers might just like or dislike the design of a table or the taste of a coffee for example. In order for good producers to keep investing in and developing their ethical programmes, or to spur the less good to improve their dodgy practices, it can be helpful to know how important the ethical position is to their customers. Although producers should be doing the right thing anyway (see 4.3), differences of opinion in management teams can sometimes see ethical elements pushed aside in favour of other goals, no matter how mission-driven a particular business likes to think it is.

1.8.1 Communicating to the manufacturer is important in cases where there is not an ethical label

For some products with a lot of ethical labels, it can be obvious that this is one of the main drivers to purchase; but this may be less obvious in other cases. In Sections 4.9 and 5.9, we discuss how some big companies and public buyers use seminars or formal education programmes to explain to their supply chains what they want. For ordinary consumers, this kind of communication more commonly involves tweeting or emailing a company or simply talking to a shopkeeper. For everyone else, it will be somewhere in between.

1.8.2 Communicating to other people is a useful way to increase the ethical activity

If people or organisations explain to other people that they are supporting a particular boycott, for example, this can be a useful way of both communicating the existence of the campaign as well as giving other people confidence that this kind of activity is worthwhile. This also applies to positive buying choices. In the various sections, we look at how some larger institutions can also explain about their ethical buying preferences in published documents or on websites.

1.8.3 Sometimes it is not about power but about awareness raising and moral argument

Although acting collectively is always best, one conversation can change another person's way of thinking. Under Section 2.6, we look at the idea of 'discrete ethical purchasing', of which vegetarianism is probably one of the best-known examples. Having a discussion about right and wrong should rarely have negative consequences (see 10.5).

1.8.4 There is a balance to be found between being boastful and being too discrete

In the second decade of the 21st century, a series of commentators (usually on the political right) began to use the expression 'virtue signalling' in a pejorative way. Although this use appears to have not survived, it was bizarre that people should be offended by moral opinions or actions. Nevertheless, there is also a long-held belief that being boastful is not an attractive trait either. Within the world of buying ethically to create positive change, being too discrete can reduce impact

1.9 Sometimes ethics on its own can't tell us what the right product is and we will need to examine our political priorities

Sometimes ethical decision-making around product choices is not straightforward. For example, if there are only two products and one has a better carbon impact whilst the other puts less toxics into the environment, ethics will not on its own be able to solve the puzzle of what the right environmental answer is (other than not to buy it in the first place). It can only be answered by deciding which issue is most important to you or which problem you think needs to be fixed first, or in other words, what your political priorities are.

This particular question arose in the late 1990s for some people when considering whether to buy a diesel car (allegedly lower carbon) or petrol car (less poisonous to humans). It also commonly flummoxes supporters of organic food – is it better to buy food from a local farm (lower carbon transport impacts) or certified organic food (less pesticide use) from another country?

This is a critical issue in ethical purchasing and applies not just to environmental choices. For example, a choice can sometimes be between one producer with a progressive approach to workers' rights but a poor approach to environmental issues and another which is good for the environment but poor for workers. In each case, it is a matter of deciding on political priorities. Often, as discussed later, part of the solution can involve joining campaigns to persuade one producer to improve in a particular area or indeed for regulators to step in and sort it out.

It is however one reason why it is necessary to treat environmental life-cycle analyses or assessments (LCAs) with caution. Asking which product has the lowest environmental impact will always run up against this problem, and only those LCAs which are open about this in their methodology and provide a variety of answers will be of any use.

For example, some of the first LCAs to appear in consumer markets compared the environmental impact of disposable nappies (diapers) with washing and reuse of cloth nappies. Unsurprisingly, those sponsored by the disposable nappy industry felt that carbon impacts were most important, and they pointed out that energy used in washing reusables was apparently higher than in the production of disposables. LCAs from the other side took a different view and focussed on the use of timber and cotton in production and disposal. This is why it always makes sense to maintain a critical mindset (see 10.5.3) and to ask questions about the origin and funding of different pieces of advice and research (including this one!).

References and notes

1.1   See e.g. Singer, Peter (1975) *Animal Liberation*

1.1.3 For authors, see Peter Singer (2002) *One World: The Ethics of Globalization.* Yale University Press. New Haven; and Pogge, Thomas (2002) *World Poverty and Human Rights.* Polity. Cambridge. For a world religions approach, see www.global-ethic.org. For the UN, see e.g. www.unsdglearn.org/courses/toward-a-global-ethics-in-achieving-the-sdgs. For academia, see www.birmingham.ac.uk/research/activity/globalethics/index.aspx

1.3.2 Ethical Consumer publishes a global directory of ethical consumption organisations at www.ethicalconsumer.org/research-hub/global-directory-ethical-consumption

1.3.4 An archive of surveys of ethical consumer behaviour is maintained and published on the Ethical Consumer website in its research hub. It is summarised in the chart of consumer opinion. It also has details of surveys looking at Brazil, China, and so on.
       https://research.ethicalconsumer.org/ethical-consumption-opinion-survey-archive

1.4.3 Branded! How the 'Certification Revolution' is Transforming Global Corporations by Michael E. Conroy, 2007, looks at diamond industry self-certification.

1.5.1 Lisa A. Neilson (2010) Boycott or buycott? Understanding political consumerism. *Journal of Consumer Behaviour*, 9(3), p. 214.

> The Ethical Consumer Research hub has 20 years of UK retail ethical market size measurements archived there. www.ethicalconsumer.org/research-hub/uk-ethical-consumer-markets-report

1.5.2 Distinguishing between expressive and instrumental boycotts are a feature of Monroe Friedman's work, including Consumer Boycotts (1999), Routledge.

1.5.4 See e.g. https://fairtaxmark.net/business-backs-eu-fair-tax-payer-label-2/

1.6.2 www.theguardian.com/commentisfree/2018/jan/31/preston-hit-rock-bottom-took-back-control – for wearing tartan if the buyer wants me to.

1.6.2 Brent Spar: see e.g. William B. Werther and David Chandler (2006) *Strategic Corporate Social Responsibility: Stakeholders in a Global Environment*. Sage. California.

1.6.3 See e.g. Roger A. Dickinson and Mary Carsky (2005) The Consumer as Economic Voter, in *The Ethical Consumer*, Edited by Rob Harrison, Terry Newholm and Deirdre Shaw. Sage. London.

> Alabama Bus Boycotts. See e.g. N Craig Smith (1990) *Morality and the Market*. Routledge. London.

1.6.4 Vietnam war. See articles cited in 10.3.1.

1.7 Surveys on ethical buying. See Harrison, Newholm and Shaw (2005) *The Ethical Consumer*. Chapters 7 and 12.

1.8.4 *The Spectator* (18/4/15). The awful rise of 'virtue signalling'.

1.9 Nappies. See e.g. *Ethical Consumer* magazine. Issue number 16. October 1991 at p 10.

2

PRINCIPLES FOR ORDINARY CITIZENS

From a chronological historical perspective, it was spontaneous actions by consumers or ordinary citizens angered by misguided business decisions which lit the spark under the fire that has become a movement for ethical purchasing. Academics have long worried that the notion of the consumer is problematic and that individuals should think of themselves primarily as citizens. These are notions which we look at in a bit more detail later (2.7 and 10.5). For the time being, we just need to note the issue and also note that the two terms will be used interchangeably in this chapter, largely to reflect the natural usage which has grown up in this area.

2.1 An individual consumer's purchases in a mass market won't make much impact on its own

Surveys tell us that this fact is so self-evident that it prevents many people from taking action at all, and that people can feel powerless and insignificant in the face of giant global brands. This is why co-ordinated collective actions, such as those discussed below, are such an important feature of so much ethical consumer behaviour.

DOI: 10.4324/9781003200185-2

Nevertheless, not all our actions as consumers are with big global brands. It is sometimes said, for example, that 20 families can keep a village shop afloat and that such choices can sometimes be ethically motivated.

In addition, in Section 1.8.3, we observed how sometimes it is not always about power and that sometimes change can also come through awareness raising and moral argument.

2.1.1 Thousands of collective actions have sprung up around markets to try to pool people's purchasing power to address ethical issues

Well-developed global collective actions where purchasers play a key role are now working across commodity markets where there are particularly severe problems of sustainability or social justice. These would include projects like Forests for All, Forever (Forest Stewardship Council [FSC] certified) and the Marine Stewardship Council. There are also projects for specific products such as tea or computers (see Chapters 8 and 6).

In addition, there are country-specific initiatives such as the Modern Slavery Act in the UK or the campaign group Conscious Consumers in Australia.

When you start to catalogue these, as we have been doing at Ethical Consumer Research Association for many years, they run into the thousands.

2.1.2 The primary actors driving these collective actions have been 'NGOs' or 'CSOs'

Political observers created the term 'pressure groups' in the 1950s to describe organisations set up to achieve particular political goals but which were not political parties. Since then, the terms Non-Governmental Organisations (NGOs) and Civil Society Organisations (CSOs) have become preferred, not least because for some like Oxfam political change is only one small part of what they do. The expressions are used interchangeably in this book.

As mentioned in 1.4.3, CSOs have learned to create market campaigns in addition to their more direct political work calling for regulation, primarily because it has come to be seen as an effective additional way to drive change as well as to raise awareness about complex issues with members and supporters.

There are two main types of collective action working with consumers: boycotts and positive buying campaigns; and principles around these are looked at in more detail in Sections 2.2 and 2.3. The way that CSOs work on market campaigns have a chapter of their own (Chapter 3).

2.2 Consumer boycotts involve withholding money as an act of disapproval

Boycotts are the earliest example of ethical market campaigns. Ostracism or turning your back on someone as a form of moral disapproval is as old as recorded human history. Self-evidently, refusing to give your money to people you believe to be in the wrong is more forceful than simply wagging a finger, but less extreme than hitting them over the head with a stick!

Boycotts are therefore obvious and instinctive and occur spontaneously in rich and poor communities, across time, and in all the countries of the world. A boycott of a 13th-century monastic community in Britain has been recorded, as have boycotts of companies which refused to recognise trades unions in the US in the early 20th century. We have also seen boycotts of the products of British imperialists in India and China as well as a sugar boycott by religious communities in the 1850s Britain protesting against the slave trade.

2.2.1 Boycotts can range from simple expressions of local outrage to complex international collaborations

In April 1989, the worst sporting disaster in British history took place when 96 people were crushed in crowds during a game between Sheffield United and Liverpool at Hillsborough football ground. The Murdoch-owned Sun newspaper wrongly reported that Liverpool fans were to blame and accused them of a range of further criminal acts. The people of Liverpool spontaneously boycotted the newspaper and have continued to do so ever since. Despite this being a relatively local campaign, it has resulted in an estimated loss to News International of £15 million per month.

At the other end of the scale, the introduction of an openly racist set of 'apartheid' laws by the South African government led to a 32-year boycott of the country which began in 1959. From small beginnings, it grew into an enormous co-ordinated international movement, whose participants included churches, local authorities, trades unions, consumers, academics, and sports teams in most of the countries.

According to the Interfaith Center for Corporate Responsibility, between 1985 and 1990, South Africa "suffered a net capital outflow of $12 billion … and [saw] 40% of foreign-owned companies withdraw assets." Two-thirds of the US companies in the country in 1984 had left by 1991. Another source estimates that sanctions caused South Africa's GDP 20%–30% lower than it otherwise would have been.

2.2.2 Boycotts are particularly useful where there is little common ground between parties

It is not unheard of for humans to take entrenched positions, to believe fervently that the other side is wrong or misguided, and to refuse to give any ground. For example, the conflict between Israelis and Palestinians has led not just to consumer boycotts against companies actively trading with Israel or in the occupied territories, but also to counter-boycotts of companies which accede to this boycott and do not participate in this trade.

Another long-standing boycott is against the Swiss food multinational Nestlé. Campaigners believe that the company's proactive marketing of its infant formulas can lead to a reduction of breastfeeding in poorer countries with negative impacts on infant health. The company apparently believes the campaigners to be dangerous Marxists opposed to the legitimate right of companies to freely market their products. At the time of writing, the boycott is still ongoing after more than 40 years.

2.2.3 The use of boycotts has declined in the 21st century, although 'name and shame' campaigns continue to thrive

From the mid-1990s, the use of positive buying collaborations as a campaigning tactic has mushroomed. It is also possible to track a decline in boycott activity to this same period. For example, after a few years of boycotting unsustainably harvested timber, people got together to promote the purchase of certified sustainable timber via the FSC scheme instead. Positive buying campaigns are covered in more detail in Section 2.3.

Rather than running a full-blooded boycott campaign, it is often easier for civil society groups to place a story of unethical corporate behaviour in the public domain and see what happens. In many instances, a company will capitulate quickly without the need to focus on direct economic impact. Sometimes it will even capitulate before the story is published, if given the chance (see 3.2.1).

Some campaign groups, Greenpeace in particular, nowadays prefer this 'name and shame' approach of highlighting poor performing producers. This is the tactic they have used around unsustainable palm oil production in Unilever and Nestlé supply chains since 2007. Approaches by campaigners to boycott campaigns are discussed in more detail in Chapter 3.

2.2.4 In some senses these two types of action are indivisible in markets with many choices

It is also worth noting that boycotts and positive buying campaigns both necessarily involve elements of the other in their operation. If there are ten types of coffee in your supermarket and you positively choose a Fairtrade organic one, you are also effectively 'boycotting' the other nine. From the other point of view, if you are 'boycotting' a particular multinational coffee company and still buying coffee, you could be said to be positively choosing another brand.

2.3 Positive buying campaigns encourage particular purchasers to make ethical choices

Positive buying is an expression used to describe the selection by a purchaser of a particular product because of claims of a superior ethical impact. And although companies marketing their products with ethical claims have a long and not always glorious history, the emergence of huge global collaborations in this space, such as the Fairtrade and Organic movements, has more recently displayed a new and highly successful approach to growing innovative production models for the future. We know for example that in the UK, Fairtrade-labelled bananas accounted for 36% of all sales in 2012 and Organic baby food for 44% of all sales in 2006.

Most Western consumer markets now have at least some producers trying to claim superior ethical impacts, and many of these will try to use a label or logo or to work with NGOs to promote this claim. Positive buying campaigns around ethical products are now the most common type of collective ethical purchasing action.

2.3.1 *Greenwashing is a well-recognised problem in this space*

In the early 1990s when positive buying was just beginning to be understood as a phenomenon, companies were naïve around what they could get away with. In a classic early case of greenwashing, the oil company British Petroleum decided to promote itself as a 'green' option, famously changing the colour of its branding and logos too. It was not long before newspaper headlines such as 'Green BP fells rainforest' (for an oil pipeline in Colombia) suggested to its directors that perhaps this wasn't one of the cleverest rebrands ever seen.

Although greenwashing has not gone away, it has become more subtle (see corporate labels below). It has also been joined by a range of other less well-coined expressions such as 'bluewashing' (pretending to uphold the values of the UN) and pinkwashing (pretending to support breast cancer elimination).

2.3.2 *Ethical labels or logos have become a key element in positive buying campaigns*

Ethical labels have become a key way of helping consumers to identify products and services making a wide variety of ethical claims. Like boycott campaigns, labels may be applied to products (e.g. Fairtrade) or to companies (e.g. B-Corporation). In 2017, the Ecolabel Index was the largest online directory of ethical labels tracking: at that time, 464 labels in 199 countries and across 25 industry sectors. There is a whole chapter on Ethical Labelling Schemes later on in Chapter 8.

Consumer surveys, predictably perhaps, find that consumers would prefer fewer and better ethical labels. Like political parties though, people have found it easier to set up many small factions than to agree general principles in a few broad groupings. In some cases, setting up competing schemes appears to be a deliberate political tactic created by companies to try to control and often reduce the ethical standards expected of them (8.3.1).

2.3.3 *The quality of ethical labels varies*

Pretty much any company can dream up an ethical logo and add it to its packaging without recourse to anyone else. Ethical labels may also be sophisticated international collaborations, led by civil society groups with transparent and regular impact measurements such as the Fairtrade label.

This means that ethical logos can appear on a spectrum ranging from complete greenwash at one end to transformative global movements on the other (see also 8.3.3).

Rather unhelpfully, ethical labelling is not normally regulated by governments. There are a tiny number of notable exceptions such as Organic food labelling in the EU. Governments may also introduce their own schemes, such as the A-G energy labels seen on electrical products in Europe and elsewhere (see 6.6.1).

2.3.4 *Spotting the best ethical labels will usually involve looking for the involvement of trusted CSO*

The best ethical labels commonly involve 'multi-stakeholder' collaborations between campaigning CSOs and companies. Sometimes such a multi-stakeholder group may even involve trades unions (e.g. Fair Wear Foundation) or government departments.

The best shorthand for finding one that is not greenwash will be to look for a CSO whose judgement you trust which is involved in the organisation's governance. A classic case in point is the ability to distinguish between the FSC (Forests for All, Forever), which in 2017 had Greenpeace inside the tent, and the Roundtable for Sustainable Palm Oil, which most definitely did not.

There are other ways to look for quality in ethical labels. One is to look for an 'audit and certification model' which is transparent (i.e. where records are kept of physical visits to supplier factories, farms, or mines). We talk more about audit and certification elsewhere in this book (4.5 and 8.3) and will discover that it can sometimes be problematic in itself.

2.4 Telling manufacturers why they are being boycotted or bought is important

Section 1.7 states that communicating ethical purchasing choices is key to effectiveness. It explains that unless consumers tell them, a manufacturer will not always know that ethics are influencing their customers' buying decisions. In addition, if a consumer tells others that they are buying a particular product for ethical reasons, it is a useful way of both communicating the existence of a campaign or project as well as giving other people confidence that this kind of activity is worthwhile.

(a)   For positive buying:

Contacting manufacturers is especially important in cases where a consumer is choosing it because its product is perceived as relatively ethical, but there is no ethical label on it or it is not otherwise making obvious ethical claims. It is also important to tell them why. Many currently have 'contact us' forms on websites.

(b)   For boycotts:

Most current boycott campaigns will have standard messages to send to targeted companies. Campaigns will also usually encourage supporters to use social media as this approach also tells other people what you are doing and why.

(c)   In shops:

For consumers, simply talking to a corner shopkeeper can be an effective way to get them to try stocking a favourite ethical product, or indeed to de-list an unfavourite one. Much retail in the 21st century though takes place in big chain stores where the humans behind the tills have little control over the products on the shelves. Campaigners are well versed though in creating collective ways of telling bigger retailers what consumers think.

(d)   Petitions:

Petition and online campaigning websites have taken a big role in the last ten years in helping to facilitate this kind of conversation. A classic case occurred in 2016 when Lucy Gavaghan, a 14-year-old campaigner, wanted to end the sale of all eggs from caged chickens in the UK (free-range eggs took around only 46% of the market at that time). In all, 480,000 people supported her petitions on change. org working through all the major UK supermarkets (starting with Tesco's) until they had all publicly pledged to be cage-free by 2025. Incidentally, forward dates for pledges for reform are a recurring and potentially problematic characteristic of this space.

(e)   For repeat purchases:

Obviously many purchases, like toothpaste, are repeat purchases. It will clearly be daft to email the manufacturer every time this happens – "Hi. I'm still buying your toothpaste because you're still not testing it on animals" – which will soon get boring for everyone! As we discuss in Section 2.6.1b, one of the ways in which consumers can make sense of the complexity of applying ethics across all their purchases is by habitually buying the same thing.

2.5 There is also a phenomenon which we can call discrete ethical purchasing

Whilst much ethical purchasing is about driving change in a collective or political sense, there is also a significant amount of discrete ethical purchasing taking place. We know this particularly through surveys and consumer research. For example, an early survey in 1989 in the UK found an old man boycotting Japanese products because of his experience as a prisoner of war in 1945. And as discussed at 1.6.1, I was boycotting one particular shop in 1976 in Birmingham because it did one thing I disagreed with. It is possible that, in some cases, the prevalence of discrete ethical purchasing exceeds that of many collective purchasing campaigns.

It is not only personal boycotts but in positive buying too where we can see ethical issues being discretely taken into account. For example, many people buy from businesses run by friends or family because they know they need some income rather than because they particularly like or need the product that much. This looks quite like buying to support the local economy – a more formal ethical approach which we can observe local authorities taking in Section 5.2.2.

For many people, a decision to act ethically is between them and their conscience, and the existence of external campaigns and indeed the impact of a particular action may be interesting but not important. Discussions about how to live a good life or how to be a good person, sometimes known as virtue ethics, have kept philosophers busy since at least Aristotle in the 4th century BC, and are well covered elsewhere. There is no doubt that people engaged in this kind of thinking are behind much of the ethical purchasing taking place, both discrete and otherwise.

It is also, of course, possible to support campaigns discretely, without 'communicating with others', as we have suggested above. Some people, as we saw in Section 1.8.4, are also keen not to be seen as boasting about their ethical behaviours.

There are also two or three main areas where we can observe discrete ethical purchasing taking place.

2.5.1 Vegetarianism and veganism can be observed in most countries of the world

People who self-identify as vegetarian or vegan can now be observed across most modern cultures, and motivations vary widely from respect for animals to improving personal health. In many countries, between 2% and 5% of the population self-identify in this way, with India appearing to be a significant exception, where around 30% of people refrain from eating meat.

Since the majority of human meals are consumed in the company of others, the absence of meat on somebody's plate in a group is not discrete, in the sense of being hidden from view. However, it is not usually part of an organised campaign against the meat industry either, and is instead usually viewed as a personal decision which is very often motivated by ethics.

2.5.2 There is also evidence that some people choose 'low impact' lifestyles across many different cultures and times

From the Benedictine monastic orders of Europe in the middle ages to 21st-century off-grid ecological communities in England, Tibet, and everywhere in between, people have been observed living deliberately simple, non-materialistic lifestyles throughout history. There is also no doubt though that the late 20th-century realisation that, collectively, humanity was using three planets worth of resources has generated a whole host of new behaviours around low-impact living, which in many cases are clearly influenced by ethical issues. Perhaps the most frequently articulated ethical concern has been for future generations.

Much of this activity takes place at an individual rather than formally collective level, and this is why this behaviour can be labelled as discrete. Surveys, for example, show that around 30% of people in the UK are taking public transport or cycling on some trips rather than driving cars for environmental reasons. Others may be buying second-hand goods or locally produced food or solar panels for their roofs. It should also be noted that although non-materialism is as much about not buying things, it still makes sense to look at it through the lens of ethical purchasing. In ethical purchasing campaigns, boycotts of poor producers are just as important as positive buying from good ones. Low impact living could therefore also be described as a boycott of material goods or of materialism itself.

2.5.3 Some low impact lifestyles are more discrete than others

Some low impact living projects, like the Benedictines and ecologists mentioned above, are collectively organised. Although they may be discrete, in the sense they are not formal campaigns for change with goals and end points, many are consciously organised as 'demonstration' or 'model' communities. In this sense, they aspire to drive behaviour change in others by example.

It is also possible to note that some governments, with varying degrees of success, have sought to use persuasion to drive 'sustainable consumption behaviours' on behalf of their citizens (see 6.6.2). Projects engaged to work on this have tended to find that getting people to reduce impacts collectively in groups have been more successful than working with individuals. Seeing everyone else engaged in making sacrifices for collective goals is apparently key to this success.

Non-governmental initiatives, such as the Transition Towns movement, have also grown up in this space.

2.6 There is a lot of complexity in trying to look at ethics in modern consumer markets

As mentioned in 1.6.5, a mobile phone can contain more than 300 separate components, each with different impacts, and a modern supermarket can stock more the 90,000 different items from food to clothing and electronics.

If this wasn't complicated enough, we have already seen how:

(a) Different products can be strong in different ethical areas (1.8);
(b) There are a lot of ethical grey areas in the real world (1.1.2);
(c) Most people are looking at price and quality as well as ethics (1.3.3); and
(d) Supply chains stretching round the world can make it difficult to check what is going on.

A common initial response, if you read shopping bloggers at least, is to throw one's hands in the air in despair! Indeed, some of the simple lifestyles discussed in 2.5 articulate the choice of simplicity as, in part, a rational response to this ethical complexity.

However, in Section 9.7 we note how the profusion of choice in many consumer markets does mean that despite all this difficulty, ethical issues remain of interest to consumers if only to help make a rational choice between lots of products which seem otherwise identical. We also know that millions of consumers are neither simplifying (much) nor despairing (much), and are trying instead to use ethical purchasing to drive markets to become less unethical. In addition, potentially billions of them are making ethical choices in markets at least some of the time (1.3). There are four main approaches which we can observe consumers using to take shortcuts through this complexity.

2.6.1 *Four specific solutions to help with this complexity have emerged*

(a)   Ethical labels have become shorthand for many consumers:

As discussed in more detail in 2.3, an ethical label on a product can give consumers confidence that someone else has looked at the problem and tried to address it. Although this works most of the time, one problem with this is that ethical labels or campaigns are often trying to solve just one specific problem and are not always looking at the whole product or company.

For example, the 'CanopyStyle' project, which encouraged clothing companies using viscose not to use fibre from natural forests, was later criticised for not looking at the pollution production processes common to its manufacture or indeed the rights of workers in the same supply chains. Fairtrade and organic labels can also appear on the products of companies which are less ethical in other parts of the business (e.g. tax avoidance). We have also seen that there is quite a wide variation in quality of labels and their standards (see Chapter 8).

(b)   Many consumers find a brand they trust and stick with it:

As the New Economics Foundation explained in 1998:

> The main mechanism for labels (or brands) to work is not to change or make up the mind of the consumer in a shop, but to confirm an earlier decision made outside the market place influenced by marketing, the media, and crucially, civil processes.

This means that once someone has identified, for example, a toothpaste that tastes OK, is not too expensive, and is not tested on animals, they will make repeat purchases – sometimes for decades. And when they find a brand that they trust on ethics generally, such as Patagonia or Lush Cosmetics, they can buy a whole range of things from footwear to shampoo without having to recheck all the ethical details each time they choose a new product from them. This is probably the key approach which makes complexity manageable for most ethical consumers and is why many brands try hard to be seen as green or ethical – often when they are not.

(c)   *Third party advice and rankings are growing too:*

Some groups have emerged specifically to provide advice to consumers on ethics. The UK's *Ethical Consumer Magazine* is probably the best known, and in its 'Global Directory' in 2018 it listed 39 others around the world which it knows about. There are probably two main types of advice organisations in its list:

(i)   Small self-help groups of consumers which have been created specifically to address this complexity issue. For example, the Italian group Consumietici is run by 'Acea Onlus', the Association of Ethical and Alternative Fuel consumption, Public Goods and Lifestyles. It describes itself as "a voluntary association that focuses on the protection of individual rights, the promotion of ethical consumption and sustainable lifestyles, and solidarity, and the protection of common goods for public welfare."

(ii) Some of the larger mainstream consumers' organisations, formed in the 20th century mainly to provide advice on product quality and safety, have now branched out and address ethical issues too. The Consumers' Union of Finland (Konsumentförbundet Kuluttajaliitto) is one example of an organisation of this type.

In Chapter 5, we note how it can help the growth of ethical consumer behaviours if governments become involved in funding or performing ethical rankings themselves. One such example is the Austrian Bewusstkaufen project, an initiative of the Environment Department. It provides a web portal for sustainable consumption in Austria which, amongst other things, provides a quality grading or ranking of around 250 ecolabels. Ethical ranking as a tactic used by campaigners are also discussed in more detail in Section 3.5.

(d)   *Commercial websites have also proliferated in this area:*

Because consumers are looking for help to navigate this complexity, the idea has emerged of the provision of buying advice as a service. This is distinct from asking consumers to act because of a campaign for particular goals, which we have identified in Sections 2 and 3. There has been a proliferation of websites offering people the ability to buy a wide range of 'green' products online. The selection process for these products is where the service of simplification comes in. Most of these have struggled to find a business model that works in an area where the competition (mainly from the tax-avoiding, web giant Amazon) is intense. One of the longest lived in the UK is ethicalsuperstore.com, which is still hanging on in there.

(e)   *General principles can be useful too:*
Asking questions such as 'is it made locally'? or 'is it made from natural materials'? can sometimes be shortcuts to less problematic choices in this space. Unfortunately, the definition of a 'natural' material is not in itself problem-free.

2.7 Change is most effective if individuals act as citizens as well as consumers

A common criticism of the idea of ethical consumption as an agent of change is that it is the notions of consumption and the consumer society itself which lie at the heart of many Western societies' current problems. Individuals should be acting as citizens, campaigning for their governments to regulate rather than through markets where inequalities of resources (and therefore the ability to take action) are at their most stark. We also know that regulating ethics in markets can have a much greater impact when it works (see 1.4.4 and 6.1).

Whilst this observation is true, it fails to recognise some of the structural problems around regulating corporate behaviour in our current democracies identified in 1.4.2 and 10.1.3 (corporate capture and internationalisation of markets).

It also presents a false dichotomy, since people can be both citizens and consumers at the same time. *Ethical Consumer Magazine* has long printed in its footnotes: "Ethical consumerism is not a replacement for other forms of political action. But it is an important additional way for people to exert their influence." And indeed, as we see in campaigning (Chapter 3) it is not uncommon for consumer market campaigns to offer a quick intervention while people are waiting for the slow mechanisms of government to come up with effective regulation. Ethical purchasing can also help grow ethical businesses which can join in on the side of campaigners, thereby helping progress a regulatory ask (1.5.4).

We look in more detail at regulatory solutions to the problem of externalising social and environmental costs in Sections 6.9 and 10.1.

All this does of course mean that as citizens, people need to engage with their democratic representatives and political parties to make these kinds of changes happen. Conveniently, many of the campaign groups already operating in this space like Avaaz and Greenpeace make this easy to do by building collective actions to seek these goals too (see Chapter 3).

2.8 Consumers or citizens aren't always the best place for responsibility to lie

In Section 1.5.6, we discuss the principle that responsibility to purchase ethically exists at every stage in a supply chain. Consumers sit at the end of many supply chains and although that does give them some power (see 1.6), it also means that if nobody further down the chain has solved a problem, consumers (or citizens) are left to sort it out. It's like having to pick up the litter in your street because the street cleaning service was reduced as part of 'austerity' cuts. We can see many examples of 'consumers' (or citizens) being left to address issues happening throughout this book. In Chapter 4, we also look at the idea that companies should behave ethically whether or not consumers are expressing a market preference for it.

There are two main reasons why consumers may be ill equipped to address these issues efficiently: technical complexity and resources.

(a) *Technical complexity*

The problem with 'responsibilising' consumption too much is that not only is there a lot of complexity in some supply chains, but there are a lot of technical issues that arise too. The use of chemicals in agriculture and consumer products is one common source of disagreement – where industry commonly denies there is a problem, but scientists working on behalf of civil society organisations insist there is. 'What is the evidence of impact'? and 'how can cause and effect be proven'? are just two very difficult issues in this space. The tobacco industry, for example, hampered regulatory intervention for decades by exploiting this difficulty.

The genetic modification of food is another well-known technically contentious area. It has been widely adopted in the USA whilst being largely rejected in Europe. In the EU, although not banned in every case, there is a requirement to label it. Surveys showing a majority of consumers opposed to it continue to mean that few companies attempt to bring it to the market in the EU, as the label becomes, in effect, a 'don't buy me' sign. As we discuss in Chapter 6, the requirement to label is a softer regulatory intervention than a ban and therefore potentially harder for companies to use trade agreements to challenge.

(b)   *Resources*

Consumers tend to be the least well-resourced buyers in a supply chain. They have less money and time to research the ethical impacts and issues around product choices. This is obvious when applied to individual consumers, who may have a couple of spare hours on a Tuesday evening and £30 to buy some books. It is also true when 'consumers' are acting collectively. Greenpeace, for example, perhaps the biggest civil society campaign group specialising in market campaigning, has annual revenues globally of around £250 million. Most of the civil society campaigners acting in markets though are considerably smaller, often with less than ten staff. The PR and communications department of just one large company can have more than 100 staff and the revenue of most large corporations – of which there are thousands – tends to be measured in the billions. The revenue of a large city is also likely to be more than £2 billion and national governments will be measured in the hundreds of billions.

For example, when you combine the 300 components of a mobile phone with the technical complexity of understanding various mining impacts, it is clear that proper resources to track these issues will be huge – and this is just one product. This is why we argue that one useful contribution that governments can make (6.4) to purchasing ethics is to research and publish on impacts for others to use.

2.9 The use of ethical purchasing by consumers has a lot of untapped potential to improve conditions for the environment and people

Despite the principle in Section 2.8, governments and companies are demonstrably failing to act to protect people, animals, and the environment across a wide range of industries (1.4). Until they do, ethical purchasing by ordinary consumers can help slow or even reverse the race-to-the-bottom that unregulated markets can otherwise bring (see also 10.2).

2.9.1 Most consumers are only buying ethically some of the time

In 1.3.4, we noted how opinion surveys suggested that between 60% and 75% of people were buying ethically some of the time but not always.

It is not uncommon for academic commentators to use this as a reason to bemoan the flawed nature of humanity and its tendency towards self-interest. This tends to occur even before they consider other possible explanations, such as:

(a)   No alternative ethical products are available in many markets;
(b)   Some markets have ethical alternatives but they may be very expensive, or less effective, or hard to get hold of, or possibly all three; and
(c)   No campaigns have been launched to raise awareness of problems and ask for participation.

This suggests that increasing the prevalence of ethical purchasing is, to use the economic parlance, as much a supply side problem as it is a problem with the demand side. We discuss supplying ethical consumers in more detail in Chapter 9. Nevertheless, there is still a role for both encouraging a self-conscious ethical consumption movement (10.7) as well as recognising the role that formal education systems could play.

2.9.2 It is not being systematically taught in schools

In Section 6.6, we note how some governments have begun to add sustainable consumption to school curricula. Others have taught issues like fair trade and the existence of child labour in supply chains.

What appears to be missing is a simple message teaching people to beware of (unethical) cheap goods. In the language of economics (see 10.1), we talk of a tendency for markets which are competing to attract purchasers by price to externalise social and environmental costs. Children don't need to learn this, but it is useful to teach a certain suspicion of things which look too cheap. Less complex language can easily explain that it is not wrong to buy cheap goods, but it may be wise to check that they're not cheap because something bad is happening to someone or something somewhere else. Most of the ways to check if goods are OK are listed in Chapter 1.

A discussion of price can often bring with it useful discussions of poverty, social justice, and social class. For example, the idea that ethical purchasing is a middle-class luxury promoted by some commentators appears to suggest that employing working-class children in India and poisoning working-class families in China is a good way of addressing inequalities of wealth distribution in the UK.

References and notes

2.1   Surveys on making a difference; see e.g. various chapters in Rob Harrison, Terry Newholm and Deirdre Shaw (2005) *The Ethical Consumer.* Sage. London.

   See e.g. Efail Isaf village shop at www.bbc.co.uk/news/uk-wales-46816997. If an average family weekly spend is £100 and there are 20 families that gives a weekly income of £2,000. If surplus on each sale is 10%, then that is £400. If overheads are £200, then net income is £200 per week. Not a way to get rich, but potentially survivable if living costs are otherwise low.

2.2   *Morality and the Market* (1990). N Craig Smith. Routledge contains a fine history of consumer boycotts.

2.2.1 For the Liverpool *Sun* newspaper boycott, see e.g. www.vice.com/en_uk/article/nz8ez8/liverpool-vs-the-sun-how-the-city-rid-itself-of-the-uks-biggest-paper

2.2.1 For the South Africa Boycott data, see Peter D. Kinder, Amy L. Domini, Steve Lydenberg (1994) Investing for Good: Making Money While Being Socially Responsible at p. 97.

2.2.2 Israel boycott and counter-boycott history also covered well at N Craig Smith op cit 2.2.

2.3   For Fairtrade banana sales, see *Ethical Consumer Magazine* issue 136, June 2012. For organic baby food sales see Campaign (2006) www.campaignlive.co.uk/article/sector-insight-baby-food-organic-growth/537593

2.3.1 'Green BP fells rainforest'. *The Sunday Times.* 18 June 1989.

2.4   (d) see e.g. www.newstatesman.com/politics/uk/2016/09/teenager-who-beat-supermarket-giants-caged-hens-now-taking-tories

2.5   Personal boycotts Clouder and Harrison (2005) The effectiveness of ethical consumer behaviour at p 103 in Harrison, Newholm and Shaw (2005) *The Ethical Consumer.* Sage. London.

   My favourite discussion of Aristotle occurs in Russell, Bertrand (1946) *The History of Western Philosophy.* Routledge.

2.5.1 Friends of the Earth Europe (2014) Meat Atlas: facts and figures about the animals we eat.

2.5.2 Environmental travel choices. See e.g. Ethical Consumer Markets Report 2018, p. 26.

2.5.3 See e.g. the work of the UK NGO Global Action Plan at www.globalactionplan.org.uk

2.6   Tesco   stocks   90,000   product   lines: www.theguardian.com/
business/2015/jan/30/tesco-cuts-range-products

2.6.1   (a) Critique of canopy style in Changing Markets Foundation (2018). 'The
False Promise of Certification.'

2.6.1   (b) Simon Zadek, Sanjiv Lingayah, and Maya Forstater (1998) Social
Labels: Tools for Ethical Trade, New Economics Foundation.

2.6.1   (c)(ii) www.bewusstkaufen.at

2.8   (a)   Tobacco   industry   lobbying: www.newyorker.com/magazine/
1970/12/19/the-fight-to-ban-smoking-ads

Genetically modified food surveys; see e.g. Is There a Market for
Genetically Modified Foods in Europe? Contingent Valuation of GM
and Non-GM Breakfast Cereals in the United Kingdom (2003) www.
agbioforum.org/v6n3/v6n3a06-moon.htm

3

ETHICAL PURCHASING AND THE ROLE OF CAMPAIGNERS

This chapter is designed to explore how campaigners are using ethical purchasing to drive changes in company behaviour across a wide range of ethical issues. Civil Society Organisations will, of course, also want to make sure their own purchasing meets high ethical standards. This is covered in Chapter 7 'Principles for smaller companies, charities and social enterprises'.

In this chapter, we use the expression 'market campaign' to describe one that is trying to reform company behaviour in a given market.

3.1 Campaigning in markets is growing among civil society organisations (CSOs) seeking political change

In Section 1.4, we have observed how the number of campaigns and projects seeking to engage purchasers on ethical issues has increased significantly since 1990. This is commonly attributed to the growth of markets themselves, the success of this type of campaigning, and problems around regulatory capture and international regulation discussed elsewhere.

DOI: 10.4324/9781003200185-3

In the UK, for example, the Living Wage Foundation has emerged to accredit businesses meeting certain standards of pay and it is set up to encourage purchasers of all kinds to prefer certified companies. The UK Trades Union Congress was involved from an early stage. Fifty years ago, it would be difficult to imagine the UK trades union movement seeking to engage purchasers in this way to address low pay.

3.1.1 Market campaigns can complement working for regulatory changes in situations where industry behaviour is the cause of a problem

As we mentioned in Section 1.4.4, it is widely recognised that it is better if markets are made to behave ethically because governments regulate or ban unacceptable activities. We also noted however how this could be difficult in some situations, where regulators had become captured or corrupt and where the international nature of the issue made regulation difficult.

There are two advantages to running a market campaign in parallel to a campaign for regulatory change:

(a) *Market campaigns can get results quickly, often in a matter of months.* While it can sometimes take years to agree and pass regulations, for people or habitats suffering through unethical business activity, solutions are sometimes urgently required (see also 10.4).

(b) *Once campaigners have found or persuaded one or two companies to reform and become 'ethical champions', these companies can become allies in the campaign for regulatory change.* This is not least because it may now become economically advantageous for them to campaign to stop competitors undercutting them through externalising more costs (10.1). It is also useful for civil society organisations (CSOs) campaigning for regulatory change to have companies on board because many governments will give extra weight to the opinions of large economic actors. At Fair Tax Mark, the UK campaign for tax avoidance, for example, it was quite common to ask accredited Fair Tax companies to sign letters to newspapers or government departments supporting key elements in the campaign, such as a requirement for multinational companies to report income and tax paid in each jurisdiction (see 1.5.4).

3.1.2 Not every political issue can be addressed through market campaigns, but a surprising number can be

As discussed in more detail in Section 10.1, market campaigns are most obviously applicable when campaigners are trying to ask companies to stop externalising their costs onto the wider societies around them. It is appropriate generally to ask ethical purchasers to choose to pay extra to avoid, for example, 'toxic' production chains such as the state slavery and pollution in Uzbek cotton, which became widely publicised in 2003 (see also 3.2 and 4.3).

Politicising consumption has however proven useful in other circumstances, such as when trying to put pressure on governments or media or lobby groups. The South Africa boycotts of companies were ultimately trying to put pressure on the government to abandon its apartheid policies (2.2.1), even though it was also noted how some employers in South Africa could benefit from the oppression there.

Stop Funding Hate in the UK from 2016 onwards sought to apply pressure on the UK media to drop racist comment and reporting by focussing on companies giving advertising revenue to problem publishers. And in February 2018, companies working with the National Rifle Association in the USA were forced to walk away from joint ventures when the lobby group's continued defence of the freedom of teenagers to acquire machine guns in the aftermath of school shootings became obviously deranged.

Other issues apparently divorced from the ethics of production can be supported by encouraging ethical purchasers to buy from campaigning companies. Co-op supermarkets in the UK in 2018 had a successful campaign addressing loneliness amongst the elderly, for example, and Lush Cosmetics has supported refugee camps and kitchens at the edge of fortress Europe.

3.1.3 Many organisations take the opportunity to form coalitions to campaign in markets

Markets which are acting to efficiently externalise costs onto the least powerful in society will commonly affect a wide range of interest groups. This means that when trying to introduce corrective mechanisms, there may well be allies in organisations with similar goals. For example, in Canada in 2004, a coalition of faith, labour, teacher, and non-governmental organisations combined to set up the Ethical Trading Action Group (ETAG) with a goal of "advocating for government policies, voluntary codes of conduct and ethical purchasing policies that promote humane labour practices based on accepted international labour standards." ETAG member organizations included Canadian Union of Public Employees, Canadian Ecumenical Justice Initiatives, Maquila Solidarity Network, Ontario Secondary Schools Teachers Federation, and Oxfam Canada.

3.2 The process normally involves a research phase, and then a call for purchasers to act collectively to solve it

Although some ethical purchasing campaigns are blindingly obvious because the subject is already front-page news, normally it will involve creating a 'research paper' or 'white paper' documenting and recording evidence of company involvement and arguing for change. Classic papers of this type might include the Environmental Justice Foundation's (EJF) exposure of the use of forced and child labour for picking cotton under state-controlled cotton production in Uzbekistan. Another might be Changing Markets' Dirty Fashion report in 2017, which highlighted the deadly nature of local pollution in some viscose factories in Asia.

Often such research reports will also openly explore the potential to engage purchasers in a campaign and may also discuss tactics, such as those outlined below. It is not uncommon for reports into problems in markets to have a list of requests for a wide range of actors at each stage in a supply chain. These might include actions for international organisations, actions for governments, actions for retailers, actions for companies, actions for consumers, and so on.

3.2.1 Seeking a company response before going public is common for two reasons: libel and negotiation

(a)   Libel

In the 1980s in the UK, the threat of legal action for 'libel' (publishing untruths) by companies against their critics suppressed discussion of corporate impacts generally. This is because the cost of even just defending a case was beyond the means of all but the largest organisations.

One high-profile case occurred in 1996 when Marks and Spencer sued the ITV programme World in Action for suggesting it had child labour in its supply chains. The size of the award and costs (more than £1 million) had long been regarded as disproportionate and effectively closed one of the most well-known documentary filmmakers in the UK.

However, the mood around all this changed in the UK following the McLibel case, which ran for three years between 1993 and 1996. A tiny campaign group based in London had been sued by the McDonald's burger chain for a range of statements made about it on a leaflet handed out outside its stores. Although the court agreed with the company on some of the issues, it did not on all of them, and it was widely agreed that the attendant publicity that the case had attracted had been far more damaging to the company than the original action. From this point on, lawyers were beginning to advise companies to think carefully before using the law in this way, and by 2018 it was almost unheard of in the UK. This is particularly the case where a large multinational company is taking on a small civil society organisation in an action which would effectively end its operation. It can look like bullying at best.

Nevertheless, good legal advice when criticising powerful entities will normally be to seek a response from the target of public criticism. Giving a company 48 hours to respond is normally the right balance between an impossible deadline and too much notice to allow the preparation of counter campaigns.

(b)   Negotiation

Anecdotally, stories are told of campaign groups which have presented their research evidence to a company prior to launching a boycott or name and shame campaign and found that the company has agreed to all the remediation actions required of it before the campaign's launch. Obviously people never hear of such outcomes since the campaigns are never launched and they do not make it into the public domain. But since they affectively 'win' the campaign before they are started, it can be a very effective outcome, unless of course the aim of the campaign was to draw attention to a general problem in the industry or to attract supporters to a group by demonstrating its effectiveness!

Sometimes disclosing information in this way leads to empty threats, delaying tactics, or vague promises to look into a problem. It is more common by 2018 however that serious negotiations could begin, and it is sometimes from these type of negotiations that accreditation schemes can arise (8.1.2).

3.2.2 *Sometimes market campaigns focus on trying to make manufacturers more ethical, while at other times they focus on trying to make products less damaging*

Consumer campaigns against CFCs in aerosols, such as the one run by Friends of the Earth in the UK, were focussed on solving a product-level problem. Others, such as the 2018 someofus.org campaign against Pepsi's use of unsustainable palm oil in its products, are focussed on getting a whole company to find a group-wide solution for all the products it sells.

As above, the nature of the campaign will probably dictate the best approach. If consumers are the main purchasers, they often understand things in terms of brands rather than company groups and it will be best to frame things in this way. On other occasions, showing the disparity between a company's behaviour in different countries can be a way of arguing that they are being morally inconsistent and therefore irresponsible. As discussed in Section 4.2, this occurred when following the ban on lead in petrol in Europe because of the harm it was shown to cause children's developing brains, petrol companies continued to sell it in countries where such regulation did not exist.

3.2.3 *Market campaigns will normally involve choosing one or more of the three main types of purchasing campaign discussed in Chapter 2: boycotts, positive buying, and ranking*

Usually the nature of the unethical behaviour, the market it is occurring in, and who the key purchasers are will give an indication of which type of campaign is best.

Boycott or name and shame campaigns, for example, are normally simple and relatively easy to communicate – "this company is bad – don't buy from it until it changes this thing that it does." This makes them good for ordinary consumers who have fewer resources to understand complex comparisons. If governments are the main customers though, this is less likely to work since they rarely support boycotts but may be attracted by well-managed accreditation schemes.

Other markets may have ethical 'champions' – businesses or social enterprises which are already producing in a responsible way – and a positive buying campaign can combine communicating the problem with driving customers to the ideal producer. This occurred in 1993 in the UK when a Lloyds and Midland Bank boycott over 'Third World Debt' and the harm that it was causing to Southern populations called on students to open accounts with the Co-operative Bank instead.

Sophisticated rankings are more likely to be successful where the purchasers have a lot of resources to consider choices, such as in investment markets. They can be simplified for consumers too.

As discussed in Section 2.2.4, in some senses a market campaign, whatever it is called, will usually contain elements of all three types of action at the same time.

3.3 Boycotts and name and shame campaigns can have significant impact

Chapter 2, Principles for ordinary citizens, looked at the following principles of boycotts which will all be useful for campaigners to understand too.

2.2.1 Boycotts can range from simple expressions of local outrage to complex international collaborations

2.2.2 Boycotts are particularly useful where there is little common ground between parties

2.2.3 The use of boycotts has declined in the 21st century, although 'name and shame' campaigns continue to thrive

Campaigners may also want to note the following two additional principles.

3.3.1 Boycotts have a strong record of success with difficult international issues

As we noted in Section 1.4.2a, globalisation of production has made regulatory intervention more difficult. For some factory workers in Indonesia in 1993, for example, it was clear that their autocratic government was more concerned with attracting international businesses than it was with the rights of its own people working in their production plants. Regulatory intervention looked unlikely, so they began to reach out to European and American development and human rights campaign groups to seek support for a campaign to improve conditions in factories producing for Western brands. When it came to identifying a target company (see Section 3.7) there was one obvious and high-profile contender.

In the 1990s, Nike had developed a reputation as the archetypal modern company with no factories of its own and a penchant for outsourcing manufacturing across international borders to poorer countries in Asia where wages were low, trades unions not recognised, and working conditions poor. When it initially claimed that poor conditions were not its responsibility, an international consumer boycott emerged which eventually led to serious economic impacts. Nike revenues fell by 16% in the last quarter of its 1997–98 financial year, and its share price, which peaked at $73 in February 1997, fell by 57% to £31 in September 1998. By 2000, the company had committed to independently monitor social audits across its supply chain and it began publishing audit details on its website. The boycott was called off and this approach to managing workers' rights issues in supply chains became the benchmark to which similar global manufacturers either aspired to or were pushed towards by pubic campaigning. The high profile of Nike's brand, its "Just Do It" strapline and its ubiquitous tick logo, had provided the ever-creative non-governmental organisation (NGO) networks with opportunities for much of their usual barbed wit. Naomi Klein's No Logo contains a list, including "Just Don't," "Justice, Do it Nike," and the "Swooshtika."

It would be wrong to suggest that the 'code and audit' approach is not without its problems (see Section 4.5), but it was a salutary lesson to companies denying responsibility, and has led to improvements in some areas.

3.3.2 *Being economically effective is not always the same as being politically successful*

The campaign to end whaling provides another classic example, like the Nike boycott, of a boycott being undertaken where weak or non-existent international regulation is unable to enforce ethical behaviour across global supply chains. When fishing fleets from Iceland continued whaling in the face of international opposition in 1988, a Greenpeace-led boycott of Icelandic fish products took hold internationally. With lost sales estimated at $29 million annually when whaling revenues were running at around $4 million, the Icelandic government capitulated that year and the boycott was called off. However whaling resumed soon after, and despite an agreed international moratorium on whaling at the International Whaling Commission, ships from Iceland and Japan at the time of writing unfathomably still choose to 'harvest' these intelligent creatures.

Academics have now developed a language which helps explain how boycotts may be 'effective' without being 'successful'. This boycott, over the longer term, would fall into just that category.

3.4 Positive buying campaigns can propose more ethical models of production

Section 2.3, on positive buying for consumers, explained how "positive buying is an expression used to describe the selection by a purchaser of a particular product because of claims of a superior ethical impact." It went on to explain how "the emergence of huge global collaborations in this space – such as the Fairtrade and Organic movements – has displayed a new and highly successful approach to growing innovative production models for the future."

It also explained how ethical labels or logos have become a key element in positive buying campaigns and how labels may be applied to products (e.g. Fairtrade) or to companies (e.g. B-Corporation). It also mentioned how, in 2017, the Ecolabel Index was the largest online directory of ethical labels tracking; at that time, 464 labels in 199 countries and across 25 industry sectors.

It also went into some detail about how the quality of ethical labels varies hugely, and that greenwashing is a well-recognised problem in this space.

3.4.1 Positive buying campaigns aim to use ordinary competitive market pressure to encourage change

The goal of a positive buying (or market) campaign will usually be:

(i)   To demonstrate that a different method of production is both commercially viable and popular with purchasers; and
(ii) To use ordinary competitive pressures to persuade an increasing number of producers to produce in this way.

If purchasers can be reminded of the moral dimensions of the supply chain in question, and then directed to producers addressing these issues effectively, these positive producers will in theory increase their market share. Once other companies see this happening, and see their own market share declining perhaps, they will look at how they can be involved in solving the issue too.

The classic area of study where this first occurred was in Fairtrade-labelled coffee in the UK. With the initial success of a tiny CSO-supported brand (Cafédirect), bigger companies sought to join in.

The ideal outcome is for companies to start competing on ethics without the intervention of CSOs, and then campaigners can step away and watch standards improve (see Section 3.8).

3.4.2 *A positive buying campaign requires two things: standards and a producer to work with which meets them*

(a) If campaigners have identified a problem, let's say pollution in factory effluent, they need to work out and list the actions which a company needs to take to solve the problem. In the case of pollution, this might be the adoption of one or more new technologies or production systems and the testing of emissions.

Such standards, as discussed in Section 8.2.2, can sometimes develop into the foundations of an accreditation or labelling scheme. They may become very complex, such as the Fairtrade movement's more than 77 standards for different commodity types.

(b) A positive buying campaign needs at least one good producer to direct purchasers to. Often the most innovative ethical companies are small or even microbusinesses. This can create practical issues in offering a viable alternative with sufficient reach (availability) and at a realistic price and quality. As discussed in Section 1.3.3, most purchasers buy using price and quality as their first and second criteria, with ethics third in line. It should be noted though that, despite all this, working with small businesses has been very successful in the past (see Cafédirect and the Greenfreeze story at 3.4.3).

Sometimes big companies are available to partner with positive buying campaigns – often after a bit of work clarifying their positions and tidying up their supply chains. This was the case, for example, with the hardware retailer B&Q PLC and the launch of the (then) FSC label in the UK. B&Q had almost 40% of the UK DIY market at that time (see also 8.1.2).

3.4.3 *Where there is no best practice to drive customers to, CSOs may need to step in to create a company or product themselves*

In some instances, where companies have been reluctant to engage, new-start ethical businesses designed to work with specific positive criteria have been key. The UK social enterprise Cafédirect, for example, played a vital role in the early years of the Fairtrade movement in the UK. It was set up by Oxfam with the solidarity trading organisations Traidcraft, Equal Exchange, and Twin Trading, and was the first coffee brand in the UK to carry the Fairtrade label.

Another hugely successful intervention occurred in 1993 when Greenpeace wanted to challenge fridge manufacturers to change their core technology from one which used damaging greenhouse gasses (hydrofluorocarbons [HFCs]). When no manufacturer would even trial a 'GreenFreeze' model, claiming that there was no market, Greenpeace found a small East German company willing to take a risk and told its own supporters the story. They had 70,000 pre-orders in a matter of weeks, and within a year, most of the major manufacturers began to offer Greenpeace's propane gas-based products. In 2018, the majority of consumer fridges in Europe are now made this way.

3.4.4 Working on positive buying campaigns has led some CSOs to become involved in ethical labelling schemes

The best ethical labels commonly involve a 'multi-stakeholder' collaboration between CSOs and companies and an 'audit and certification model'. They are discussed at length elsewhere in this book, but particularly in Chapter 8.

One key theme is that this is a highly politicised space, though not one that is always articulated as such. There are pitfalls for CSOs here because, as mentioned in Section 2.3.3, the quality of ethical labels varies and CSOs can risk their reputation by backing the wrong ones. The presence of World Wide Fund for Nature in the Roundtable for Sustainable Palm Oil is a case in point and has been the source of not a little criticism.

3.5 Publishing ethical rankings can be an effective model for creating pressure

3.5.1 Ethical rankings tend to focus on all companies in a particular market

The Environmental Investigation Agency's (EIA) Chilling Facts campaign, for example, began in 2008 and ranked the UK's seven largest supermarkets on the climate change impact of their refrigeration and cooling systems. Its initial research, published in 2009, had shown that as much as one-third of a supermarket's carbon footprint was coming from the cooling gases in its refrigeration systems, and that just 14 stores across the UK were using only 'climate-friendly' technologies. The campaign's goals were specifically to get supermarkets to move away from using HFCs as a refrigerant gas.

By the second ranking in 2010, 46 supermarket stores were running on climate-friendly refrigeration and companies were beginning to make promises about future action. By 2011, 239 stores were using 'climate-friendly' refrigeration. Such was the success of this campaign that it was rolled out to 13 European supermarkets in 2013.

3.5.2 Rankings will commonly involve a numbering system or score

If there are quite a lot of factors to consider, then a score can be a good way to add up performance across a few different areas. It is also quite easy to use formulas to 'weight' numbers and give greater importance to one of two key factors.

For example, the Canadian coalition ETAG, discussed in 3.1.3, ranked clothing companies out of 100 when it published its 'Revealing Clothing: Transparency Report Card' in 2006.

Other benchmarking projects have used A to F score system (see Greenpeace Greener Electronics), or have chosen to group companies together in conceptual categories like 'making some effort' or 'nothing to say' (Labour Behind the Label: 'Change Your Shoes' 2016).

3.5.3 A regular cycle of updating can keep pressure up and reward improvements

Greenpeace's Greener Electronics rankings began in 2006 and ranked mobile phone and PC manufacturers like Apple and Samsung. The goal was to encourage the elimination of toxic chemicals in manufacture and end-of-life recycling. The guide was updated every three months, and companies and commentators could watch and discuss who was rising and falling in the charts each time round and why. It ran in this format for six years until 2012 and was instrumental in persuading companies to establish programmes to systematically monitor and address issues raised by Greenpeace. During the course of the project, new criteria were introduced, such as using renewable energy and not lobbying against environmental regulations. It was revived in a slightly amended form by Greenpeace USA in 2017.

Not all groups have the resources of a Greenpeace to be able to publish quarterly updates, but many (such as the EIA's refrigeration project) try for annual reviews.

3.5.4 Rankings work because they engage companies with familiar ideas – competition, measuring performance, and reporting

Ethical Consumer Magazine in the UK (see Section 2.6.1c) has ranked companies across a wide range of issues since 1989. While I was editing it, it was not uncommon to receive phone calls from companies or their lawyers to complain about their position in the rankings. Questions such as "what do I need to do to get more points than XX?" would reveal that it was often just the relative position against a close competitor that was driving the interaction. Of course, many companies failed to engage at all, but for those that did openly, it was clear that they were sometimes driven by a competitive spirit to be 'better' than a close rival. On other occasions, companies working hard on their ethical reputation would want to know how to get to the top of the list, whilst others would be keen to find out the minimum they needed to do to move up from the very bottom.

There is no doubt that rankings work with the kind of measurable factors, regular reporting, and competitive demands that most managers within large firms instinctively understand. This is a key element in why they can be such an effective way at both communicating very specific campaign goals and driving change.

3.5.5 Rankings can be holistic or very specific

For single-issue campaign groups, it makes sense that rankings focus on very specific areas like we have observed in the EIA refrigeration ranking above. Technical issues in a single supply chain can be sufficiently complex that producing an effective ranking around one issue and communicating it effectively is challenging enough.

The problem with very specific rankings is that companies at the top – which are by implication recommended to purchasers – may be very bad at something else. In Greenpeace's Greener Electronics ranking, they were always careful to add a rider at the bottom of each table saying this guide "does not rank companies on labour standards." It would appear however that praising companies' toxics performance when they were very poor on climate lobbying became too much for Greenpeace and a ranking on this additional issue was added at a later date.

We have also observed how other campaigning organisations such as Ethical Consumer and RankABrand have tried to produce 'holistic' rankings that brought in as many issues as possible – often by consolidating more specific rankings.

Throughout ethical purchasing, there is tension between a desire to produce one big simple answer and the practical need to urgently address some very specific problems. This tension is also present in the design of ethical labelling schemes, and is discussed in more detail in 8.4.3.

3.5.6 Transparency rankings are the most rigorous method but can miss key elements

In order to create the most effective rankings, it is ideally necessary for companies to co-operate and disclose detailed information about their supply chains. It is therefore common for ranking projects to contact companies asking for data. The trouble with this approach is that many companies may simply refuse to co-operate. At Ethical Consumer, for a new ranking, we found that a response rate of 40% would be good. If you publish a ranking containing only those companies that co-operate:

(a) It may not be very useful to purchasers – imagine a mobile phone ranking without Apple or Samsung?
(b) It can appear to reward non-co-operation for the companies who co-operated and are now at the bottom of this list.

The solution which generally works best, and that is now applied across most ranking projects, is to rank on transparency rather than on actual performance. Has the company got a policy on its website on say 'brominated flame retardants'? Does this policy have dated and quantified future targets for elimination? Does it report on progress towards these targets?

This approach has the additional advantage of being methodologically rigorous and therefore defensible legally should a formal challenge arise.

Of course, the disadvantage of this approach is that companies may be very good at being transparent, but less good at actually solving the problem in question. To some degree, an effective transparency ranking should be able to pick this up, but it can still sometimes mask genuinely poor performance.

3.5.7 The World Benchmarking Alliance

In 2017, one of the most complex alliances of organisations yet seen in this field launched a new league table of 98 global companies ranked against internationally recognised human rights standards. The project, five years in the making, was backed by:

(a) Eighty-three investment companies managing £5.3 trillion (twice the size of the UK economy);
(b) Governments of the Netherlands, the UK, and Switzerland; and
(c) NGOs, including Oxfam and ShareAction.

In time, the alliance plans to publish annual reviews of the rankings of the 500 biggest companies in the world. During the launch event, the key role played by consumers in trying to reverse the race to the bottom and the demonstrable effectiveness of league tables as a mechanism for change were referenced by the speakers more than once.

The possibility that governments could fund benchmarking projects because of the social good that would result is also raised in Section 6.6.1. The World Benchmarking Alliance uses the UN's Sustainable Development Goals as the basis for its ranking criteria (see Appendix 1).

3.6 Identifying where purchasing power lies is the normal starting point for developing a campaign

3.6.1 Market campaigns usually first involve identifying which purchasers have influence and then seeking their support

The underlying assumption of many campaigners working in this space is that you only need to persuade one key actor in a supply chain to adopt an ethical position for the desired consequences to occur. In some markets, these will be ordinary consumers – and so appealing directly to them via mass media to support best practice producers and avoid worst works best. Many campaigns of this type are discussed in this book (see Section 2).

In other markets, companies themselves have a lot of influence. For example, with Greenpeace's Icelandic fish boycott, discussed in 3.3.2, they decided to target supermarkets (the UK's main fish retailers) as the biggest UK buyers of this commodity. They could have focussed on consumers, processors, or even regulators (governments or international lawyers) to achieve the same goals. Many campaigns target retailers in the first instance, as they are most sensitive to consumer concerns and may be keen to take action before publicity becomes too intense (see 3.2.1).

In other cases, it is local authorities and public purchasers that have the most influence. Campaigners trying to drive up sales of the FSC label (see 8.2) worked hard to secure public procurement rules in the UK which specified that the supply of sustainable timber should be sought (see also 6.5).

3.6.2 Sometimes market campaigns can target banks financing particular projects

Where a damaging project has the support of a territory's government, affected communities may seek to target high-profile companies involved. For example, the role of Barclays Bank in the proposed funding of the controversial Narmada Dam in India was highlighted in a campaign by Friends of the Earth in 2004.

From 2015 onwards, a range of successful campaigns have also targeted banks supporting new coal projects in an era of increasing concern about climate change. By 2018, following publicity campaigns targeting banks with consumer brands, companies joining the pledge not to continue this practice included ING and BNP Paribas. It was recognised at the time that campaigning was only one element in helping secure the pledges, as the coal industry itself was becoming unattractive financially due to increasing regulation too. Producing lists (or rankings) of banks involved in funding fossil fuel projects was also one element of this campaign.

In 2017, in the first campaign to target insurers, anti-coal campaigners also began to target insurance companies involved in insuring new coal plants.

Sometimes this can also involve targeting the downstream 'purchasers' of bank services which will be ordinary consumers for high street banks. Some investors may also have consumer products (e.g. insurers investing in coal companies).

3.6.3 Sometimes this can involve targeting institutional investors

The South Africa boycott campaign was adept at targeting institutional investors in projects or companies active in the country. A common target of its campaign was institutions sensitive to such appeals, like charities, churches, or public bodies.

Another common target is pension funds, whose beneficiaries are the same ordinary people we know that like to see ethical behaviour.

ShareAction in the UK waged a long 'greenlight' campaign against pensions fund asking individual members to tell their own funds to take their responsibilities to address climate change more seriously.

Steve Waygood, an important figure in the UK ethical investment movement, wrote a book called *Capital Market Campaigning* in 2006 addressing this subject, which still has relevance today.

3.7 Identifying a specific producer to target for an avoidance campaign is also usually effective

3.7.1 Commonly ethical problems are industry-wide

Very often, unethical behaviour by companies can be embedded across whole industry sectors. Low wages and poor working conditions in clothing factories is just one example. If campaigners try to drive change by just telling the story of these problems, there is no obvious role for purchasers. Some trade unions have taken the view that this is the best approach, as to name and shame an individual producer can risk job losses at the company in question should the campaign become effective. Curiously though, given the point made at Section 2.4.4, this objection doesn't normally extend to positive buying campaigns (e.g. Fair Tax Mark and Living Wage Campaigns).

3.7.2 Focussing on a single high-profile brand in the first instance often makes for a more easily communicable story

The Nike boycott campaign, mentioned extensively above, is just one such example. When the campaign began, there was little evidence that Nike was significantly worse in its disregard for workers in its supply chain than its competitors at that time such as Adidas, Reebok, and Puma. Nike was chosen as a target because it had the highest profile, with a business model that had a huge advertising budget, and the fastest growth. It was also foolish enough to publicly claim that working conditions were not its responsibility.

In some cases, focussing on two or three brands in a complex market can make sense too. In the UK in 1992, the Lloyds and Midland boycott campaign chose to address the development impacts of 'Third World Debt' through a consumer market campaign. Retail banks holding such debt extended across most of the sector. They chose to focus on the two banks with the highest levels of sovereign debt in order to give consumers more practical options should they choose to support it.

3.8 Once a political issue becomes well known in a particular market, companies can begin to compete to out-do each other as more ethical

In the UK, we have definitely been able to observe this phenomenon in two main sectors – food retail and coffee Supermarkets, often targeted by campaigners because of their wide range of goods and impacts, have had periods where they have tried to compete on ethics. One classic example occurred when the UK Supermarket Sainsbury ran full-page adverts in newspapers in 2013 in response to a Tesco's advert which claimed lower banana prices. The Sainsbury's ad simply had a picture of two identical bananas side by side with the words "Same Price. Different Values" underneath it.

With smaller companies in the coffee market, once many others became certified as Fairtrade, it was difficult to stand out, and so the 'super-ethical' brands began to pursue 'multiple certifications' by getting an organic and other labels as well.

This key principle of ethical purchasing is discussed elsewhere (10.8.2), but is perhaps the ultimate goal of campaigners. If companies begin to compete on the ethical issue raised, then in a sense campaigners can step away and let 'ordinary' competitive pressures drive standards up instead of down.

References and notes

3.1.1 (c) www.theguardian.com/politics/2015/dec/15/meps-should-support-a-fair-tax-payer-label

3.1.2 During the anti-apartheid boycott of South Africa many US companies adopted the 'Sullivan Principles' to show that they were not benefiting from racist workplaces.

NRA boycott; see e.g. www.newsweek.com/nra-boycott-full-list-companies-have-cut-ties-gun-lobby-over-florida-shooting-819050

3.2 Environmental Justice Foundation (2005) White Gold: the True Cost of Cotton.

3.2.1 Independent (28/9/98) www.independent.co.uk/news/world-in-actions-pounds-2m-libel-pay-out-1201073.html

3.2.1 Vidal, John (1997) McLibel: Burger Culture on Trial. Macmillan.

3.3.1 Ethical Consumer Magazine, May/June 1992 – Nike Inc. Injustice in Indonesia Fall in revenues at Nike; see Michael E Conroy, op cit, 1.4.3

3.3.2 For Iceland whaling boycott, see Ívarsson, Jóhann Viðar (1994). Science, Sanctions and Cetaceans.

3.4.3 *Guardian* 2/2/04, Cafedirect takes ethics to the city: www.theguardian. com/environment/2004/feb/02/fairtrade.business

3.4.3 Edwin R. Stafford Cathy L. Hartman (2005). Greenpeace's 'Greenfreeze Campaign' Hurdling Competitive Forces in the Diffusion of Environmental Technology Innovation in Ahead of the Curve Cases of Innovation in Environmental Management. Springer at pp. 107–131.

3.4.4 Jordan Nikoloyuk, Tom R. Burns and Reinier de Man (2010) The promise and limitations of partnered governance: The case of sustainable palm oil, *Corporate Governance* 10(1), pp. 59–72.

3.5.1 https://eia-international.org/wp-content/uploads/Chilling-Facts-3-FINAL.pdf

3.5.2 ETAG (2006) Revealing clothing: Transparency report card https:// en.archive.maquilasolidarity.org/issues/csr/transparency/TRC/2006

3.5.3 See: www.greenpeace.org/usa/reports/greener-electronics-2017/

3.5.7 See e.g. https://corporate-citizenship.com/2017/09/21/world-benchmarking-alliance-just-another-ranking/

3.6.1 Whaling campaign; see www.greenpeace.org/india/en/story/2891/operation-breakthrough-the-story-behind-big-miracle/. See also, Tesco and Birds Eye referenced in Harrison et al. (2005) op cit 1.7 at p. 93.

   Timber procurement: www.chathamhouse.org/sites/default/files/field/field_document/20140908PromotingLegalSustainableTimberBrackFinal.pdf

3.6.2 Barclays Narmada; see e.g. www.business-humanrights.org/sites/default/files/reports-and-materials/Big-Deal-Dec-2005.pdf

   New coal funding campaign was a campaign of banktrack.org at a website called www.fossilbanks.org/

   Campaign on coal an insurance: https://unfriendcoal.com/wp-content/uploads/2018/11/Scorecard-2018-report-final-web-version.pdf

3.6.3 South Africa boycott; see Kinder et al. (1994) Op cit 2.2.1.

   Shareaction: https://shareaction.org/resources/the-green-light-campaign-using-pension-power-to-protect-our-planet/

3.7.1 See e.g. www.industriall-union.org/why-boycotting-brands-wont-help-garment-workers

3.7.2 www.independent.co.uk/news/business/lamb-lies-down-on-banks-1577769.html

3.8 www.thedrum.com/news/2013/07/31/sainsburys-release-same-price-different-values-ad-campaign-reaction-asa-ruling-over

4

ETHICAL PURCHASING AND THE ROLE OF MULTINATIONAL COMPANIES

The growth of multinational corporations in the post-war period, and the social and environmental damage that some of them have caused, has been one of the key drivers behind the rise of the civil society campaigning that we discuss extensively elsewhere in this book. Strangely enough, as a result of this campaigning, some multinational corporations have become sophisticated ethical purchasers themselves. As we will see later, the value of some of these new-found ethical purchasing systems is hotly contested. This chapter charts the rise of all these phenomena.

4.1 Purchasing, where supply chains stretch across many countries, has increased significantly over the last four decades

In Section 1.6.6, a supply chain is described as "an expression used to describe each step in the often complex process of bringing modern products to markets." We use the example of a shirt, where a cotton farmer may sell cotton to a weaver, who sells to a sewing factory, who sells to a high

DOI: 10.4324/9781003200185-4

street retailer, who sells to a consumer. Each of these steps may take place in a different country with different rules and regulations and, over the last four or five decades, this type of purchasing has increased significantly. There are four main reasons for this:

4.1.1 Purchasing has increased since 'outsourcing' to supplier companies has proven economically efficient

In the period before the 1970s and the 1980s, it was more common for multinational companies to be what economists call 'vertically integrated'. This meant that they tended to own all the companies in their supply chains wherever they happened to be. Much of this was to do with quality control issues. However, in the 1970s, it became clear that another model was possible. A multinational company could simply own a brand, a marketing department, and a purchasing function and buy in everything else it needed. Nike was in many ways the poster child for this model, and is discussed at greater length elsewhere in this book (3.3.1 and 4.2.2). And although not all other businesses have ceased to own any suppliers at all, it has now become the norm for most global businesses to own far fewer elements in their supply chains. The car industry is a classic example of this with many thousands of 'just in time' supplier companies making up complex networks around each region. This outsourced model requires less capital and is more 'nimble' in terms of making changes or adjusting to new market conditions. Others note that it is a way of passing economic risks down the supply chain.

4.1.2 Purchasing globally has increased as tariff barriers have tended to be reduced

Although the rise of Trump and Brexit in 2016 signalled a backlash to this trend, the main direction of travel over the 40-year period prior to this was unmistakeably in the direction of reducing trade barriers. The World Trade Organisation was set up by 124 countries with a mandate to do just this and carried on the work of an earlier post-war treaty with similar aims called the 'General agreement on tariffs and trades' (GATT).

The dominant economic argument of this time was that everyone would benefit from this. This argument was one element in a 'new' economic doctrine called 'neoliberalism', not least because it focused on 'liberalising' markets from barriers and regulations generally.

As we discuss in Chapter 10, one of the flaws in this theory was that it didn't recognise ethical issues as important or significant in any way. It may be instructive to speculate on whether the 2016 backlash would have occurred had this theory been more developed in this respect.

4.1.3 Technological innovation has also played a part in the globalisation of supply chains

There is much evidence from economists that, for example, standardisation of shipping containers and the mechanisation of loading and unloading at ports around the world have enabled the physical flow of goods across borders to increase significantly. The revolution in information technology has also played an important role.

4.1.4 Poor regulation around the climate impacts of fossil fuels has also played a role

Green economists have also long pointed out that transport in the oil age has not reflected the real costs of burning oil (climate change and air pollution) because these have been effectively 'externalised'. It is therefore possible to argue that artificially low prices of oil have made it cheaper to produce good at a distance in some cases and played a part in the globalisation of production too. More is written about the problem of externalities in 10.1.

4.2 Many of the problems which civil society campaigns have tried to address were to do with the absence of an effective legal or moral framework for globalised supply chains

Prior to the growth of civil society campaigns in the 1990s, multinational companies generally maintained the line that they obeyed the law in all the countries in which they operated. Whilst this was actually untrue in many cases, even when it was true, it led to some very clearly egregious outcomes. For example, when leaded petrol was banned in the West once it was found to be damaging children's brain development, companies continued to sell it in the global south where regulation had not yet caught up. The same process occurred with high tar cigarettes and many dangerous pesticides.

This approach also created problems for environmental protections and workers' rights. If discharging some specific chemicals into water is banned in one country, it can become cheaper to move production to less regulated environments than to fix the problem. Polluting paper factories using the 'kraft process', for example, were known to have been dismantled and relocated in the global south where regulations on toxic discharges had not caught up. In the same way, if workers' rights, particularly union membership, can be avoided, it can lead to cheaper production costs.

Such decisions did not occur sporadically, but in competitive markets, they occurred systematically, leading to what campaigners called a 'race to the bottom' (the company with the lowest standards wins). This is also discussed in more detail in Chapter 10 (10.1.4).

Of course, international treaties were also beginning to try to introduce rules in this space and the International Labour Organisation (ILO), for example, is mentioned below. Enforcement though can be patchy and rights of individual citizens to appeal non-existent.

The growth of civil society standards, often linked to ethical labels, has therefore been a key element in attempts to create a moral framework for production and is one of the central themes of this book. They are covered extensively elsewhere in Chapters 3 and 8. Campaigners have mainly been trying to build a new framework around two core ethical principles: ethical consistency and responsibility.

4.2.1 Northern consumers expect workers' rights and consumer and environmental protections to be given equal respect wherever the supplier

The examples above, of lead in petrol and dangerous pesticides, led some Northern development charities to create 'name-and-shame' campaigns in the country of origin of the multinationals concerned. In many other cases, discussed throughout this book, campaigners have called on consumers and companies to help as well.

Child labour in supply chains is a good example of a 'consistency issue' commonly finding its way onto the front pages of newspapers in the West. Arguing that it is culturally tolerated in many countries of the world rarely wins an argument with Northern consumers (see e.g. Primark in 4.2.2). Fortunately, around labour rights, the ILO's history of treaty making and standard setting has produced a clear benchmark around which most campaigners and companies find a workable system.

4.2.2 Consumers are expecting corporate responsibility to stretch all the way to the end of the supply chain

In Section 1.6, the basic principle that "purchasers have power where there is a choice between producers" is discussed. Below, it is the related principle that 'responsibility to purchase ethically' exists at every stage in a supply chain (1.6.6).

The classic case where this principle was illustrated was during the Nike boycott (over working conditions at its suppliers) in the 1990s. It took a seven-year-long international consumer boycott with some measurable economic impacts before Nike was persuaded that it could not get round this principle by outsourcing. This campaign is discussed in more detail in Section 3.3.3.

Companies have complained that they sometimes have little impact with a particular supplier as their order is only relatively small. Or they have also pointed out that they have clauses in their contracts which do not permit a supplier to subcontract further to other suppliers with lower standards. These arguments look weak when the abuses revealed are significant. In 2008, the BBC's flagship current affairs TV programme *Panorama* revealed that manufacturers in Primark's supply chain were employing child labour from Sri Lankan Tamil refugee camps to sew sequins on clothing. From a reputational risk management point of view (see Section 4.3.1), it did not help Primark that such clauses existed in its contracts or that its order was small. Viewers were persuaded that it was its job to know what was going on right to the end of its supply chain, and if what was going on was bad, it should stop.

4.2.3 Some Southern voices have argued that applying these kinds of values is a form of cultural imperialism

Arguing that Western ethical values in business are a kind of cultural imperialism is not uncommon. This is sometimes a position taken by government officials used to taking bribes for permitting a transaction to take place in countries where this is openly tolerated. Occasionally, it also occurs in other ethical areas such as a requirement for independent trade unions in some Asian countries, or for child labour to be defined as young people over 16 years of age.

Sometimes these look more like economic than cultural arguments. "Your countries cut down all your forests and employed children in your factories when you were developing, then why shouldn't we?" is one line that has been taken.

Generally, most people recognise that though there may be a small element of truth in some of these arguments, for a company to use them to justify, for example, employing slave labour or children under the age of eight would be extremely unwise. Respecting fundamental human rights has been one of the cornerstones of effective international collaboration.

4.3 Much formal ethical purchasing at bigger companies developed initially as a risk management response to the emergence of civil society campaigning

Big companies will often tell you that they always act ethically irrespective of what is happening elsewhere. However, most formal green procurement programmes and supply chain human rights monitoring appear to have emerged a couple of years after civil society campaigning around that particular issue began (see e.g. Nike). It can therefore be easier to understand them as a response to this new phenomenon.

When Ethical Consumer Research Association began formally looking for such initiatives in 1989, they were few and far between. There was almost no Corporate Social Responsibility (CSR) reporting and very little evidence of formal management of workers' rights protections in supply chains.

The proposition that ethical purchasing at bigger companies was initially responsive is even more clear when collective initiatives are observed. The arrival of the online social audit checker SEDEX (see 4.4.1) and the Better Cotton Initiative, which appeared in 2005 as a response to campaigning around problems in the cotton industry particularly, are just two examples of this.

4.3.1 *After this initial period, CSR programmes and ethical purchasing became more systematic and can now generally be characterised as risk management*

The rise of consumer boycotts in the 1980s and the 1990s (2.2), and the learning that the potential support for such campaigns could extend to as much as 70% of the general public (1.6.2), led larger companies – particularly those with consumer-facing brands – to view these as a serious risk to their businesses. Coupled with this were additional pressures around ethical behaviour from some investors and governments. Mitigating business risk in a formal way is something that management teams are familiar with.

Issuing formal CSR reports to persuade people that a business has spotted a particular issue and is dealing with it in a responsible way became the initial response to this. Many were very poor and became famous for their large colour photos of pristine landscapes. Since then, the quality has improved somewhat. This is partly due to collective initiatives such as the 'Global Reporting Initiative' (GRI) whose standards many larger companies now use (see also Appendix 1 and 4.6.3).

Ethical or sustainable supply chain management nowadays generally appears as a subset within CSR programmes. For manufacturing companies though, particularly those using problem ingredients like cotton, palm oil, or conflict minerals, it can be where the majority of their 'reputational risk' lies.

It is common to see high-risk companies nowadays try to identify and mitigate risk before civil society does. They will normally have formal programmes which are systematic and predictive, often prioritising actions within complex programmes commonly over long time frames (e.g. a five-year plan). Some common criteria used are covered in Section 7.4.

4.3.2 *The likelihood of future regulation has also been a major driver of change*

Generally, when environmental consultants come knocking, they will tell a company that it's necessary to develop a responsible management programme because:

(a) Customers will increasingly demand it. This is the main subject of this book;

(b) It is likely that regulators will eventually get round to banning or restricting the problem activity. This means that the work of solving it will need to be done anyway, and to do it earlier makes a company look like a leader instead of a laggard.

As we can see in Section 3.7.1, these two drivers will most often be interconnected. Campaigners will be persuading consumers or other purchasers to address an issue at the same time as lobbying governments to intervene.

It should be noted that elsewhere in this book, we also discuss some of the structural problems which make government intervention difficult (see e.g. 1.4). This means that other solutions like requiring transparency (see 6.6.1) may be adopted.

4.3.3 It is possible to observe some exceptions to this responsive approach for some company types

With millions of companies trading globally, there are of course many exceptions to this generalisation that CSR and ethical supply chain management emerged largely as a responsive phenomenon. They can perhaps be divided into three main types:

(a)   Co-operatives and some social enterprises

In some countries, co-operative supermarket groups grew in the 20th century to become significant food retailers with turnovers in the billions of pounds. In the UK and Switzerland particularly, when the Fairtrade movement was emerging, they became early champions of some of the first Fairtrade products, helping to create scale and wide distribution for a nascent movement.

(b)   Privately owned companies with a leadership that was not exclusively focussed on the bottom line

In the UK, the Body Shop was the classic example of a company trying to do things differently. There have since been many others. In the period before its ill-fated (from an ethical point of view) public floatation, its charismatic founder Anita Roddick showed how trading and campaigning on social issues could be merged into a single organisation.

(c)   State-owned monopolies

British Telecom, for example, was a state-owned company privatised by Margaret Thatcher's government in 1984. It had a formal 'Green Procurement' programme in 1992, which appeared to be a hangover from the time before it was privatised and when it was free to consider social and environmental goals without the pressures of market competition. Very little else like it was around in the UK, at least at that time.

More about the growth of mission-oriented company types appears in Section 10.9.

4.4 Collective actions, both positive and negative, have proliferated in this space

As we have seen elsewhere in this book, there has been a big growth of civil society campaigns and collective initiatives to try to address social and environmental impacts of global business. These include both boycotts (2.2) and positive buying campaigns (2.3).

In response to this, businesses themselves have also set up new groups and collective projects to help them navigate this area. On a practical level, solving deep-rooted social and environmental problems can be technically complex, and businesses can pool resources to increase efficiency. In this section, we break down these initiatives into three main types.

However, we have noted elsewhere the essentially political nature of this space (8.3). This means that we can characterise some if these initiatives as negative rather than positive, as they appear to be attempts to undermine or reduce standards rather than to enhance them. Of course, industry itself would not characterise them this way at all. For them, they would be an attempt to refocus the debate away from the unreasonable and uneconomic demands of undemocratic campaign groups!

4.4.1 With industry

The Supplier Ethical Data Exchange (SEDEX) is an online platform set up in 2004 for manufacturing companies to publish or share their social audit reports from previous factory visits. With the explosion of interest in the idea of auditing suppliers for workers' rights compliance at that time (4.5), some factories were receiving more than 30 different visits a year from separate buyers groups. It became clear that there was a lot of duplication of effort and that some sort of central repository made sense. Although not without its critics, the not-for-profit group has since grown into a big operation with more the 50,000 companies using it annually.

Another collective initiative is the Electronic Industry Citizenship Coalition which was formed in 2004 by a group of major multinationals, including Sony, Apple, and HP. It was originally set up to create a common set of standards for workers' rights in their supply chains, although it later embraced other pertinent issues like conflict minerals and expanded beyond the electronics industry. Its standards were, perhaps carefully, chosen to be less than what campaigners wanted, but better than nothing!

In the UK, and probably many other countries, we have a Chartered Institute of Purchasing and Supply which provides formal training in 'procurement'. Although quite early on they were providing advice on sustainable procurement, it has clearly been quite difficult for them to provide bipartisan technical advice in an area as intensely political as this.

Finally, there are collective business approaches which we could characterise as 'cynically undermining' higher standards. Of course, in public, everyone is very polite in this space and people are entitled to a range of different standards if they choose. However, it is the inescapable conclusion that this appears to be the purpose of some schemes. The Programme for the Endorsement of Forest Certification (PEFC) is a classic example of this, and is used elsewhere in this book. It was a sustainability certification scheme set up by forestry companies in 1999 after the emergence of the (then) Forest Stewardship Council (FSC) in 1996. Unlike the FSC, there is no facility for civil society scheme members. There are many other examples, including the Indonesian Sustainable Palm Oil and Malaysian Sustainable Palm Oil schemes (8.3).

4.4.2 *With civil society*

As we discuss elsewhere in this book, one of the key responses to the problem of ethics in global supply chains has been for civil society to form 'multi-stakeholder' partnerships with businesses. These will commonly involve an ethical label or accreditation scheme so that consumers and other purchasers can see that particular products have been supplied with these issues in mind. The Fairtrade, organic, and FSC schemes are all examples of areas where such partnerships have been formed. These schemes will tend to have some kind of assurance or audit model, whereby practitioners will actually visit production sites in supply chains to check what is really going on. We discuss the code and audit model in more detail in Section 4.5. We also discuss such schemes under 'ethical labels' (2.3.3.1) in the chapter for citizens, under positive buying campaigns (3.4) in the chapter for campaigners, and in Chapter 8 generally.

It is possible to conceive of such schemes sitting on a spectrum where at one end, the schemes are dominated by campaigners and at the other they are dominated by companies (8.3.3). The organic scheme is an example of a more campaigner-led scheme and the Rainforest Alliance scheme an example of a more company-led approach.

The presence of companies in such schemes is essential for their success, though it is useful to be aware of a tendency for larger companies to create pressure to keep standards low within such collaborations or, as they would characterise it, practical.

4.4.3 *With governments*

Some governments, aware of the wider benefits of ethical purchasing, have become involved in schemes to promote it amongst larger companies.

In the UK, the Ethical Trading Initiative (ETI) was set up in 1998 to bring campaign groups, trades unions, and companies together to address the problem of workers' rights abuse in supply chains which stretched into 'less developed' countries. It was formed by the Department for International Development partly because a case was made that if companies paid a living wage, for example, then less development aid in cash might be needed. They were also influenced by the rise of consumer boycotts against UK companies at that time, partly driven by a highly active campaign group culture in the UK. They reasoned that it made economic sense to try to get all the parties round a table to find a mutual solution, if possible, before a campaign was started. Since then, they have become an established part of the landscape, mainly providing training and collaborative space for companies to help address the very difficult practical issues that come from applying ethical standard in real world situations. We also look at the ETI and a US equivalent FLA, in Section 6.8 (under Governments).

Where companies (and indeed government purchasers) are working around consensual ethical issues, there may be opportunities to purchase collaboratively to reduce price. The World Resources Institute in the USA, for example, has a 'Best Practice Guide for Collaborative Solar Procurement'. They have also looked at buying green power more generally with the Green Power Market Development Group in the USA.

A footnote to this section is to observe that generally collaboration by businesses over, for example, price is seen as illegal in most legal systems. This unfortunately can be a problem for collaborations to address ethical problems and is discussed in more detail in Section 10.2.4.

4.5 Codes of conduct and supplier audits have emerged as a way of managing workers' rights issues in multinational supply chains

4.5.1 Third party audits of company ethical claims have increased substantially over the last 30 years

Capitalist societies have learned that to create a culture of trust around financial reporting, it is a good idea to get an independent third party once a year to 'audit' the financial records of a company to make sure they are telling the truth about how much money they have really made. This does go wrong from time to time, such as the now famous quasi-criminal collusion which was revealed in 2001 to be occurring between the auditor and the audited at the US energy company Enron. However, with the occasional regulatory correction needing to be introduced, the system has generally functioned more or less effectively.

The rise of concern around ethical as well as financial issues in markets that occurred in the second half of the 20th century has seen the idea of getting in an independent third party to audit ethical claims that companies make too. We can observe this developing to some extent in the annual 'sustainability' or 'CSR' reports that large companies put out. For example, PricewaterhouseCoopers has verified the environmental data published by Bayer, Mitsubishi, and Unilever, amongst others, in the past.

However, where it has really caught on is in the supply chains of multinational companies, and in particular around the management of workers' rights issues.

4.5.2 The code and audit model for managing workers' rights problems in supply chains has been particularly prominent

As we have seen elsewhere in this book, the main driver of concern over workers' rights has been to avoid the risk of being 'exposed' in a TV documentary as a company employing workers in exploitative 'sweatshop' conditions, and then becoming the target of consumer boycott campaigns. Proven allegations of long hours (in excess of 60 per week), pay that is too low to live on, dangerous working conditions, and child labour have impacted materially on the reputations and financial position of brands around the world.

At first, campaigners called on companies to sign up to 'codes of conduct' for workers' rights, and much was made of the need to include a range of key clauses such as 'freedom of association' (to join trades unions) and the avoidance of child labour. Although multinationals initially rushed to sign up to such codes, it soon became clear that signing up was one thing and applying it in practice was another.

The solution appeared to be found in sending in teams of specialised production site auditors and a huge industry has now grown up around this. From tea plantations to garment manufacturers, social audit teams are regularly visiting and formally reporting on what they find. In 2011, Wal-Mart, for example, hired auditing firms to conduct more than 9,800 separate factory inspections. And large companies, such as SGS, Intertek, and Bureau Veritas have also moved into this space. It is big business. Much has been made of this new layer of 'civil regulation' which appears to be filling a gap in regulation and enforcement around some issues globally (see Section 8.6.3). However, the model has also been heavily criticised.

4.5.3 *The code and audit model is not without its critics*

Just like Enron, the social audit model has had its high-profile scandals. The 2012 Tazreen fire and the 2013 Rana Plaza factory collapse, which both occurred in Bangladesh and where more than 1,000 people lost their lives, occurred in factories which had 'passed' social audits. And it is also well known that some company groups have maintained 'model' factories for Western inspectors, whilst 'subcontracting' much of the work to other factories in the group they are less keen on auditors seeing.

While such high-profile cases are illustrative of a systemic problem, and indeed the tendency for corruption and greed in the human world, just as Enron on its own was not a reason to abandon financial auditing, audit fraud is not necessarily a reason to abandon the whole idea of third party social audits. Much has been written by academic and other commentators about this subject, but there appear to be two particular problems that the social audit model needs to address to remain credible.

(a)   Co-ordination between buying and CSR departments in the same company is not commonly enough

    Whilst many Western consumer brands are now demanding that supplier factories meet their 'codes of conduct' regarding respect for workers' rights, at the same time the buying departments of the same companies may be haggling on the price for delivery of 5,000 garments next month. For the factory owner, with sales targets to meet, there is rarely any doubt which of these voices speaks louder, and it is on the social side where cuts are made. This means that for some areas of workers' rights which don't cost too much to ameliorate, like the provision of basic health and safety equipment, social audits have been evidenced to be in general effective. For other areas which cost more to fix, such as the provision of a living wage, the audit model does appear to have made little impact. What is needed is for companies to make a real commitment to minimum ethical standards and to integrate this into buying arrangements throughout the supply chain. Many companies acknowledge this now, and a very few are making progress, but there remains much to be done. Training buyers in ethical programmes is certainly the key to one of the locks on this door.

(b)   *Tackling difficult issues is also necessary*

It is clear from Ethical Consumer's studies of thousands of companies operating audits in this area that for many of them it is a box ticking exercise. When the code and audit model starts to reveal problems, for some companies, there is a tendency to look away.

The classic example in this area, and indeed a bit of an elephant in the room, is the fact that almost all codes will have clauses requiring 'freedom of association', or in other words, the right for workers to join trade unions. However, in China, the biggest single global manufacturing location for many industries, free trade unions do not exist, in the sense like they are understood in Europe and the Americas. The same is the case, at the time of writing, in some other countries such as Bangladesh and Belarus.

For a very few companies, such as Levis, for a while at least, this kind of issue has meant not sourcing from Chinese factories at all. Others have tried to address the problem in creative ways such as by using the 'parallel union' ideas suggested within collective programmes like the ETI (see 4.4.3). For most though, it appears that where their codes and business interests clash; it is a code that takes second place.

Ethical Consumer has developed quite a detailed list of requirements for what is likely to indicate a good supply chain management programme for workers' rights such as unannounced audits and the presence of non-governmental organisations (NGOs) on the auditing team. There are other difficult issues it identifies such as the subcontracting of work to 'home workers' where poor rates of pay and long hours have been common throughout history.

SEDEX (4.4.1) also has an 86-page document containing Best Practice guidance for ethical audits, which suggests a wide range of processes to help address a similar range of difficult issues.

4.6 Environmental or green purchasing by multinational companies is better than it was but still needs work

In the early 1990s, when companies first began to look at the idea of green purchasing, some of it was quite embarrassingly poor. Banks, for example, would report on how much recycled paper and low energy light bulbs they had bought whilst overlooking the impacts of core areas of the business like lending to environmentally destructive mines and dams.

To some degree, the story of major companies coming to grips (or not) with their environmental management belongs elsewhere rather than in a discussion of purchasing. Much manufacturing is still based on owning factories and employing staff, and so addressing environmental impacts in these situations will be less about ethical purchasing and more about environmental management. However, there is increasing acknowledgement in environmental management circles that addressing supply chain impacts is key, as we will see below.

4.6.1 Raw materials like palm oil or cobalt also have impacts which need addressing at the purchasing level

Even where a company owns its own manufacturers, it is likely that they will purchase at least some raw materials from suppliers or commodity markets. As we have seen elsewhere in this book, many environmentally problematic raw materials collective projects and third party accreditation schemes have been set up to help companies to 'green their supply chains'. Companies may therefore be asked by stakeholders to buy FSC timber or Roundtable on Sustainable Palm Oil-certified palm oil. In other cases, there may be business collaborations short of accreditation which perform a similar purpose such as the Better Cotton Initiative. We have also seen elsewhere (2.3.3), how in some cases such schemes themselves can be criticised, so they are commonly only part of a solution.

We have also seen with the code and audit model for addressing workers' rights that problems can occur with schemes with agreed ethical standards if there is no co-ordination with a company's buying department (4.5.3).

In addition, there is anecdotal evidence that a focus on price by companies within multi-stakeholder initiatives can also lead to lobbying for a reduction of standards.

4.6.2 Best practice for carbon measurement and disclosure now involves looking down to the end of supply chains

The Carbon Disclosure Project (CDP) was described as the "most powerful green NGO you've never heard of" by the *Harvard Business Review* in 2010. Originally founded in the UK in 2002, it now works with more than 6,000 multinationals as well as hundreds of cities and states to get them to publicly disclose their carbon emissions and then to manage them downwards. They claim that this amounts to roughly 20% of all human-derived carbon emissions.

Early on in the project, it became clear that supply chain emissions were key, and according to the CDP, carbon emissions located in supply chains are on average four times higher than a company's own direct emissions. The CDP started by giving a better score to companies which disclosed emissions down to their second- and third-tier suppliers. Now they have a formal 'Supply Chain Programme' which, among other things, has a central reporting mechanism for more than 11,000 suppliers, which works in the same way as SEDEX does for workers' rights (4.4.1).

The CDP now uses this framework to collect data on deforestation and water-related risks, too.

4.6.3 Best practice sustainability reporting requires some acknowledgement of supply chain impacts too

The GRI is another Three-Letter Acronym operating in this space! It has been very successful in designing standards for 'sustainability reporting' for companies and its framework is being used by more than perhaps half of all large multinationals as well as governments, small and medium-sized enterprises, and NGOs in more than 90 countries.

As part of its Environmental Standards suite of eight standards, including materials, energy, and waste, is GRI 308 (2016), a 'supplier environmental assessment'. There is a similar 'supplier social assessment' standard called

GRI 414 (2016). The breadth of GRI's adoption has led to it being criticised for creating a framework which is easy to use at the expense of one that has depth and impact.

Similar concern and work around supply chains, if not formal processes yet, exist within other collective reporting programmes like the UN Global Compact. As mentioned above, a list or GRI reporting areas appears in the Appendix (A5).

4.6.4 Greening supply chains normally involve some kind of Life Cycle Analysis and management plan

As we discussed in Section 3.4 (and in 4.4.3), prioritising key areas for action helps to give structure to an environmental management plan and indeed an ethical purchasing programme.

In order to understand where the most problematic impacts occur for the production of physical products, it is normally necessary to undertake some kind of life cycle analysis or life cycle assessment. These will look at each stage of a product's life cycle such as extraction, production, manufacture, distribution, use, and disposal/recycling.

Although scientific methods can be very good at measuring and quantifying critical impacts at each stage, it can not necessarily help with prioritising each area when different products are better in different areas (as we saw in Section 1.9, basic principles). There is also a problem with this kind of analysis of where the 'system boundaries' are drawn. If you use iron in your product, for example, do you look at the manufacturing impacts of the diggers and mining trucks at the extraction site or not? Mike Berners Lee at Lancaster University found that these kinds of issues might create nearly tenfold difference in various assessments of the carbon impacts of common product like burgers.

Whilst such assessments should still be carried out, there could probably be a greater degree of honesty towards their limitations in company literature.

4.6.5 The idea of regenerative purchasing is beginning to challenge the idea of sustainable purchasing

Recently, there has been an increasing understanding of how social and environmental regeneration can take place in communities or ecosystems which have become degraded. The idea that supply chains could be regenerative is an offshoot of this kind of thinking. Sustainability takes as its assumption that if humans don't make things worse, then it should be OK for future generations. In some ecosystems though repair is already needed; so sustaining it at its current level is not enough. Lush Cosmetics is one activist company (see also 9.9) working in this area and a range of collaborations such as Regeneration International are beginning to emerge too.

4.7 Supply chain transparency is becoming an important way of addressing criticism

The idea that transparency can rebuild confidence in unpopular organisations is a key theme in both ethical purchasing and the study of political institutions generally.

4.7.1 Where supply chains are particularly controversial, some companies are now publishing lists of their contracted factories or suppliers

When controversies arise, many companies will try to reassure civil society campaigners that whilst they may acknowledge a general problem, their own supply chains are problem free. "If this is the case," say campaigners, "why don't you tell us who your suppliers are?" "It's commercially confidential," say the companies. "If we told you, all our competitors would discover our secrets and be able to produce this stuff too."

Generally speaking, this argument is looking weaker over time. This is partly because producing thousands of items with an obvious logo on in factories with hundreds of people in is a difficult secret to keep. If TV companies can find out what is being produced in a factory, then so can a reasonably resourced competitor. In addition, many producer factories are proud of their contracts with big multinationals and will advertise this on their websites when they are looking for business. 'We produce for global brands including Tesco and GAP' is not an uncommon thing to read. This argument is also looking weaker, because some very large companies have now been actually publishing their supplier lists for a long time and the sky has not fallen on their heads.

As we have seen elsewhere in this book, clothing supply chains and the problem of sweatshops are one of the most publicly discussed problem areas for global business. A recurring theme here is that the global boycott of Nike in the 1990s was where key lessons were learned for both businesses and campaigners. It was also the time when it became obvious that the emerging Internet was a place where a lot of detail could be published at minimal cost. Nike was therefore one of the first global brands to publish a list of its factories on the Internet (which is still online today). It has since been followed by other huge clothing brands like H&M which uses an online interactive map to name its suppliers and also lists them down to the second tier in some cases.

In other controversial supply chains like palm oil, campaigners have been successful in persuading companies to produce supplier lists. Unilever and Nestlé, for example, which between them buy 4% of global palm oil supply, published their direct and indirect supplier lists in February 2018 after significant campaign pressure.

Not unexpectedly, the publication of supplier lists has not, on its own, meant that controversies have gone away. Nike, H&M, Nestlé, and Unilever have all been revealed to have had ongoing problems with particular suppliers even after the publication of these lists. It might therefore be said that publication of supplier lists is a necessary but not sufficient step in the right direction.

4.7.2 New technologies have made tracking and transparency of supply chains more practical

Radio-frequency identification chips, bar codes, and blockchain technology have all been tried out as approaches to track products and their ingredients from one production stage to another. Once a company knows what is going on, it can choose to share this more widely. Historic Futures, for example, is a UK company which has specialised in using technology to help big UK retailers track what is happening inside their own supply chains. Walmart (ASDA in the UK) experimented with them in using maps to show the supply chains of jewellery, clothing, and food for some specific products.

The flip side to this is that such technologies are also available to campaigners. As *Harvard Business Review* explained in 2010:

> Webcams are cheap, and iPhone apps are easy to develop. If firms don't release provenance information themselves, others will do it for them.

Scan the code, and customers will be able to see the sweatshop, the factory farm, or the unsafe working conditions - live.

Of course, you don't need new technologies to track and understand a supply chain. For example, the FSC's 'chain of custody' approach to tracing a log from a forest to a piece of furniture is largely paper-based, but just as likely to be effective.

4.7.3 Some companies are making a virtue out of transparency and using it to tell a product's story to customers

For some companies, radical forms of transparency can become selling points or differentiators (see also Chapter 9). The Swedish sustainable jeans company Nudie, for example, has a website which uses both maps and stories to share details about a garment's production and distribution, down to the grower of the cotton (an Indian NGO) to the producers of zips. And the notion of 'direct trade' (with a single-producer farm) for some commodities like tea and coffee has also encouraged the idea of telling a producer's story. The US coffee producer Counter Culture Coffee, for example, has 'partnership stories' on its website explaining its growing relationship with the Kazoza producer co-operative in Burundi. It has tended to be smaller companies rather than giant multinationals pursuing this type of approach most consistently to date.

4.7.4 Regulations are beginning to appear in this space

The UK Modern Slavery Act, passed in 2015, requires all companies trading in the UK (above a certain size) to publish a Modern Slavery Statement explaining what they are doing (if anything) to prevent the use of slave labour in their supply chains. Although it is not a requirement for companies to publish details of their supply chains, it is a form of regulation which uses a requirement for transparency to drive change. Although responses have been patchy, there is little doubt that it has forced a huge new group of companies to consider (and occasionally act on) an issue which they had assumed did not have much to do with them.

Other requirements for transparency include the requirement to disclose activities in Tax Havens imposed on European banks in 2014 (CRD IV). This discussion is continued further in Section 5.6.6.

4.8 Developing a mature attitude to cost and pricing in relation to ethics is essential

Nobody rises far in the business world without a good understanding of the need to control costs. Indeed, many have risen to the top solely on a reputation for cost-cutting. These kinds of individuals can cause immense damage to the world around them, and BP's Deepwater Horizon explosion and oil spill in the Gulf of Mexico is just one example of what can happen when health and safety measures become areas where costs can be 'saved'.

4.8.1 Sometimes changes to make a production system more ethical can actually save costs

Energy-saving measures, both in supply chains and in owned premises, are the classic example of a win-win situation for both costs and climate. Although companies were slow to catch on to this, rising energy prices mean that now very few larger companies do not now have some kind of energy management plans. Not every ethical decision is so easy however.

4.8.2 More often than not though choosing ethical behaviours may incur real costs for a business

As we saw above in discussions of the code and audit model for workers' rights at 4.3.5(a), where improving working conditions is not too costly (like provision of health and safety equipment), codes have had some impact, but when improvements are more costly (like implementing a living wage), then evidence of impact is lower. In addition, it is obvious that dealing with waste responsibly (like fitting pollution treatment equipment at the end of pipes) will tend to be more expensive than simply pumping out untreated muck into a river or sewer.

4.8.3 Business executives should be required to train in ethical decision-making

It is important to be wary of looking at ethical issues with a purely mathematical model. Ralph Nader's book Unsafe at any Speed exposed in painstaking detail how executives and designers in the US car industry in 1965 systematically avoided incurring costs on safety equipment modifications leading to measurable increases in deaths and injuries, of which they were aware.

They had openly calculated that the fines for killing people would be lower than the cost of fixing the problems. It is now regarded as a classic work and led to the creation of a new government department and regulator of vehicle safety in the USA.

If the only way to make a thing 'economical' is to make it unethically, then maybe the best decision is not to make it at all, or to make it in a completely different way. This means that sometimes cost may need to be elevated to the level of a strategic business decision.

In campaigns against unequal rewards in the garment sector, Civil Society Organisations will commonly publish a breakdown of the costs of a product showing how little (in relative terms) paying more to the workers at the end of the chain would cost. Such analyses would calculate how the cost of an across-the-board pay increase for the most poorly paid workers would compare to last year's dividends, the costs of a global advertising campaign, or even the chief executive officer's own pay packet.

If a business is to take ethical decisions which do cost money and which perhaps makes it proud of taking the right decision, then it is worth looking at whether it's possible to communicate this to customers or staff – who might like to be proud of the company too. As we see in Chapter 9, this is not the same thing as saying it is possible to charge more to a big group of non-price sensitive ethical consumers, but the value to the brand and the likelihood of consumers staying with the brand can become stronger.

4.9 Many of the general principles outlined elsewhere in this book also apply to multinationals

4.9.1 Since multinationals are often bigger than their suppliers, people generally will expect them to use their influence to eradicate unethical activities

One of the basic principles of ethical purchasing is that "purchaser power, both ethical and otherwise, is related to the size of the purchase value relative to the size of the supplier" (1.6.2).

We have seen elsewhere in this book how persuading your supplier to change can be difficult if you are a small company or individual. Multinationals will not normally have this type of problem, and their suppliers will often be much smaller. Like local authorities, their contracts are sometimes so large that they can persuade their suppliers 'to wear tartan' if they want them to (1.6.2).

4.9.2 *Helping or training suppliers adapt to new ethical specifications can be useful*

British Telecom, mentioned in 4.3.2, was one of the first UK companies to adopt supplier seminars as part of a green purchasing programme in the early 1990s. Amongst the services they offered was technical expertise to move to new, less polluting, types of equipment. Companies can also offer finance to their suppliers or longer-term contracts in exchange for adopting particular ethical approaches. Mondeleez has claimed to do this as part of its Cocoa Life supply chain programme.

Obviously, this type of approach only really works where there is a long-term relationship with a supplier.

4.9.3 *Communication is key – telling stakeholders about ethical purchasing will make them feel good*

(a)   Customers, staff, and investors

We saw in Section 4.7.3 how some companies were using supply chain transparency to tell stories about their products which can get them noticed in crowded markets. We also see in Chapter 9 how an ethical purchasing programme may not, on its own, make thousands of customers choose a product over that of a competitor. However, people that already do buy your products – and know about the ethical programmes – will be less likely to leave a brand once a competitor comes along. Some people also suggest that staff and investors can also become more loyal if they can relate to the ethics of a brand (see also Chapter 10).

(b)   Suppliers

Questionnaires and ethical requirements in contracts are the most common way of informing suppliers of ethical standards and are also covered elsewhere (3.5.2, 5.7, 5.8). As discussed above, the standards they express are the starting point for an ethical supply chain, but auditing and other measures will be necessary to identifying suppliers who just tick 'no' to everything in the hope that no one is watching.

4.9.4 *Recording and reporting on positive impacts can embed ethical purchasing programmes*

As we discuss under Sections 3.3.1, 3.7(b), 5.10, and 6.5, looking at organisations with more openly social goals, recording and measuring the positive impacts of an ethical supply chain policy can help embed it into an organisation. This kind of approach to communication makes it less likely that an ethical purchasing programme will be abandoned as soon as a cheaper competitor to an existing supplier comes along.

References and notes

4.1.1 Barnet and Muller (1976) Global Reach: The Power of the Multinational Corporations provide the classic analysis of globalisation and outsourcing.

4.1.1 Collins, Bechler and Pires (1997) Outsourcing in the automotive industry: From JIT to modular consortia. *European Management Journal* 15(5), pp. 498–508.

4.1.3 See e.g. Daniel Headrick (2009) *Technology a Word History*. Oxford University Press. Oxford.

4.2 www.huffingtonpost.co.uk (2014) Corrupt Executives Sent To Prison for Pumping Toxic Leaded Fuel Overseas

Castleman BI (1979) The export of hazardous factories to developing nations. *International Journal of Health Service* 9(4), pp. 569–606.

Race to the bottom; see e.g. www.economist.com/free-exchange/2013/11/27/racing-to-the-bottom

4.2.1 Philippe Grandjean (2013) *Only One Chance: How Environmental Pollution Impairs Brain Development*. Oxford University Press. Oxford.

Child Labour; see www.theguardian.com/business/2008/jun/16/primark.child.labour and www.just-style.com/analysis/the-highs-and-lows-of-the-latest-child-labour-violations-list_id134599.aspx

4.2.2 Primark fires child worker firms (June 16, 2008) http://news.bbc.co.uk/1/hi/business/7456897.stm

4.2.3 See e.g. https://hbr.org/1996/09/values-in-tension-ethics-away-from-home

4.3.3 (a) Fairtrade movement and the role of co-operatives; see e.g. Harriet Lamb (2008) *Fighting the Banana Wars and Other Battles*. Rider. London.

4.3.3 (c) Green Procurement Programme Report 1992. British Telecom.

4.5.2 Specialist brand risk advisors have emerged that produce publications annually looking at human rights risks in various sectors such as e.g. www.maplecroft.com/insights/

Walmart: www.npr.org/2013/05/01/180103898/foreign-factory-audits-profitable-but-flawed-business?

4.5.3 Bangladesh   audits: https://newlaborforum.cuny.edu/2018/04/17/
an-accident-in-history/
Clean Clothes Campaign (2019) FIG LEAF FOR FASHION How social
auditing protects brands and fails workers

4.5.3 (a) Clean Clothes Campaign (2005) Looking for a quick fix: How weak
social auditing is keeping workers in sweatshops

4.5.3 (b) Ethical Consumer (November 2019) Supply chain management
ranking criteria www.ethicalconsumer.org/our-ethical-ratings/people
SEDEX (May 2019) Sedex Members Ethical Trade Audit (SMETA) Best
Practice Guidance Version 6.1

 4.6 Banks' environmental reporting: Ethical Consumer Issue 60 (August
1999).

4.6.2 *Harvard Business Review* (2010) The most powerful green NGO you've
never heard of https://hbr.org/2010/10/the-most-powerful-green-ngo
Carbon Disclosure Project website (2019) www.cdp.net/en/info/
about-us/what-we-do

4.6.3 GRI details available from www.globalreporting.org.
Criticism of GRI; see e.g. Levy, D.L., Brown, H.S. and de Jong, M.
(2009) 'The Contested Politics of Corporate Governance: The Case of
the Global Reporting Initiative', *Business and Society* 49(1), pp. 88–115.

4.6.4 Mike Berners Lee (2010) How bad are bananas: The carbon footprint of
everything. Page 5. Green Profile. London. See also The Importance of
Carbon Footprint Estimation Boundaries
H. Scott Matthews, Chris T. Hendrickson, and Christopher L. (2008)
Weber Environmental Science & Technology 42(16), pp. 5839–5842.

4.6.5 Lush and regeneration. See e.g. https://uk.lush.com/article/big-refund-
faq. See also https://regenerationinternational.org/

4.7.1 For Nike's supplier details see: http://manufacturingmap.nikeinc.com/.
H&Ms   is   at: https://sustainability.hm.com/en/sustainability/
downloads-resources/resources/supplier-list.html
For Palm Oil supplier disclosure, see Greenpeace Report (2018) The
Final Countdown: Now or never to reform the palm oil industry.
For details of Nike, H&M, Nestlé, and Unilever problems with
particular suppliers, see www.ethicalconsumer.org company profiles.

4.7.2 Historic Futures and Walmart; see e.g. https://archive.fortune.
com/2009/05/08/technology/traceability.fortune/index.htm
Harvard Business Review: https://hbswk.hbs.edu/item/what-brands-
can-do-to-monitor-factory-conditions-in-a-global-supply-chain

4.7.3 Nudie   producer   stories   are   within   www.nudiejeans.com/productionguide/

Counterculture stories are within https://counterculturecoffee.com/sustainability/partnership-stories

4.7.4 Modern Slavery Act impact: See e.g. www.christianaid.org.uk/sites/default/files/2017-09/Salt-corporate_approaches_to_addressing_modern_slavery.pdf

Capital Requirements Directive IV (CRD IV): European Union (2013a) Directive 2013/36/EU of the European Parliament and the European Council Brussels.

4.8 BP Deepwater Horizon: Corporate Reform Collective (2014) *Fighting Corporate Abuse: Beyond Predatory Capitalism*. Pluto. London.

4.8.1 Ralph Nader (1965) *Unsafe at Any Speed. The Designed in Dangers of the American Automobile*. Grossman. New York.

4.8.3 For campaigning around the relatively low cost of improvements for workers, see Oxfam International (June 2018) Ripe for Change: Ending human suffering in supermarket supply chains and also https://oxfamapps.org/behindthebarcodes/

4.9.2 For British Telecom, see http://bvnews.bureauveritas.com/wps/wcm/connect/bv_cnen/local/home/news/latest-news/news-csr-british-telecom?presentationtemplate=bv_master_v2/news_full_story_presentation_v2

Mondeleez see: https://www.cocoalife.org/

4.9.3 For brand loyalty and ethics, see Anne Bahr Thompson (2017) *Do Good: Embracing Brand Citizenship to Fuel Both Purpose and Profit*. AMACOM American Management Association. New York.

5

PRINCIPLES FOR LOCAL AUTHORITIES AND OTHER PUBLIC BODIES

5.1 Ethical purchasing has proven an effective additional way for local authorities to pursue their legitimate social and political objectives

It is estimated that public sector purchasing represents between 11% and 18% of the UK's gross domestic product. It is likely to be a similar figure in other countries too, though elsewhere (like the federal arrangements in the USA and Germany) there is even greater local or state autonomy. The expression 'local authorities' is used here to refer to any regional political body, including federated states.

Like governments, it can make sense for local authorities not to make purchases in ways which undermine other goals of the organisation. For example, for organisations responsible for managing public health, it may not make sense to be investing pension fund money in tobacco companies. Or for an organisation concerned with managing regular flooding of a town or city, it does not make sense to buy its own power from coal-fired generators. In Section 5.2, we have characterised five main areas where observed institutional ethical purchasing is common. In some cases, there

DOI: 10.4324/9781003200185-5

is genuine excitement around the potential improvements to people's lives that may be possible if this approach were more widely adopted.

Like other large institutional purchasers covered in this book (companies and governments), suppliers can be keen to make changes almost instantly to secure large contracts (1.6.2). There is also a specific language that has grown up to describe purchasing in this area, which includes terms like 'contract compliance' and 'procurement'.

5.2 It is possible to observe and characterise five main types of ethical purchasing by local authorities

5.2.1 Solidarity purchasing

Solidarity purchasing occurs where regional authorities want to support a political cause outside their jurisdiction by creating incentives on supplier companies to reconsider their activities there. The classic case occurred during the global boycott of South Africa over its openly racist apartheid policies. By the mid-1960s, 54 UK councils were banning goods from South Africa from their offices and schools, many of them in Wales and Scotland. According to Richard Knight, whose book focussed on the boycott in the USA, "by the end of 1989 26 states, 22 counties and over 90 cities had taken some form of binding economic action," whilst others gave "preference in bidding on contracts for goods and services to those companies who do not do business in South Africa." More recent campaigns against other 'oppressive regimes' in Burma and Israel have also sought, and often won, local authority support.

The politicised nature of these campaigns has led many governments, who are often controlled by different political parties, to try to restrict local authorities from using their purchasing power in this way (see 5.4). This has contributed to ethical purchasing by local authorities becoming the most closely regulated form of ethical purchasing.

5.2.2 Buying locally or for local economic impact

Some studies of local economies suggest that intelligent public purchasing can have a significant impact. For example, in 2005 the UK non-government organisation (NGO) New Economics Foundation published research in collaboration with Northumberland council which showed that suppliers based in Northumberland re-spent on average 76% of their income locally, while suppliers from outside the county spent only 36% in the area.

Preston City Council in the UK is well known for having devised such a programme and for involving other public sector purchasers, including the hospital and university. In 2013, before the programme began, the six local public bodies spent £38 million in Preston and £292 million in all of Lancashire. By 2017, those totals stood at £111 million in Preston and £486 million throughout the county.

A different approach to the same problem can be seen in those local authorities which are trying to use tax avoidance as a procurement criteria. In the UK, many outsourcing or 'service provider' companies have complex offshore tax structures and a history of low tax payments. For most people it seems counter-intuitive to give public money to companies which are structured in such a way as to never give a penny back in corporation taxes. A 2016 campaign by Fair Tax Mark and Christian Aid called 'Sourced' managed to persuade a range of local authorities to sign pledges, including Manchester, Oxford, Birmingham, and the London boroughs of Lewisham, Lambeth, and Southwark. Interest in such an approach can also be seen elsewhere in Europe.

Keeping the right side of regulations has been an important, and particularly difficult, part of ethical purchasing in this area too (see 5.4).

5.2.3 Sustainable procurement

Environmentally conscious buying by local authorities, commonly referred to as sustainable procurement, is one of the most widely practised forms of ethical purchasing. A survey in 2010 looked at 280 public procurement practitioners from 20 countries and found some kinds of sustainable procurement occurring in the majority of them (Walker and Brammer). First discussed internationally in 1992 at the Rio Earth Summit and recognised as an obviously good thing to do, there is now a wide range of published guidance and advice for local authorities on how to implement such policies. In Japan, there is a law requiring all local authorities to buy sustainably and in the USA sustainable procurement has generated its own labelling systems such as the energy star label.

However, as we discuss in Section 1.9, deciding what is 'sustainable' and what is not is difficult and interpreted in a wide variety of ways, and some local authority sustainable purchasing programmes are clearly very weak.

5.2.4 Social procurement

As we discuss later in Section 10.9, the idea that social enterprise could become an important systemic solution to some of the problems created by the behaviour of profit-seeking corporations has been gathering pace. In the 1990s, Italian laws, which recognised this and allowed some buyers to prefer co-operatives in public purchasing, had to be redesigned following European rules requiring a greater focus on price. Since then, it has become increasingly clear that disadvantaging businesses which are trying to 'internalise' social costs (see 10.1) could be counterproductive, and European rules were changed in 2014 to address this. Buyers in Europe can now, for example, reserve some contracts for enterprises employing people with disabilities or other disadvantages, or which are addressing other social, health, or cultural needs. Although implementation is patchy to date, there are other developments in this space (see Section 5.9) which are encouraging.

We also note how government departments, and even the US Department of Defense, have done work on social procurement in Section 6.3.1.

5.2.5 Attention to investments and assets

As we discussed in Chapter 3, when campaigners are targeting companies to seek behaviour changes, they will often read through lists of shareholders to see if any might support their campaign. It is also common for public pension funds or even general public authority assets to include shareholdings in mainstream companies. At this point, campaigns can begin to ask them to consider either divestment (selling the shares) or engagement (asking to meet the company to share concerns).

Public authority divestment became a central plank of the Anti-Apartheid campaign (2.3.1), and more recently, the campaign to divest from fossil fuel companies has taken a similar approach. The website gofossilfree.org listed 149 government institutions as having taken some form of divestment action in 2018, including cities in Australia, Germany, Sweden, France, Ireland, the UK, and the USA.

However, it is not just solidarity purchasing which has influenced a more ethical approach to managing public authority funds and there are examples of authorities using funds to address the other main buying approaches too: social, environmental, and local economic impact. Preston County's pension fund, for example, is now building student accommodation in the city and renovating a hotel.

5.3 Ethical purchasing is also practised to a lesser extent by other public bodies and purchasing consortia

(a) Government departments are covered in Chapter 6.

(b) Universities are commonly active in solidarity movements, not least because well-informed and active students can persuade reluctant bureaucracies to take action. Naomi Klein in No Logo, for example, provided some detail about the role of US universities in the anti-sweatshop movements at the turn of the 20th century. Universities also commonly have relatively advanced sustainable procurement programmes.

Strictly speaking, many universities are independent organisations, and to some degree the sections in this book on Ethical Purchasing for larger companies (Chapter 4) or for NGOs (Chapter 7) will be useful too. But with public funding often at least underwriting a core part of their revenues, they can also be seen as quasi-public bodies to some degree.

(c) Healthcare organisations, often with huge budgets, will sometimes have at least some sustainable purchasing criteria. UK campaign group Sustain, for example, has campaigned to persuade hospitals to serve healthy organic food for many years. And the National Health Service in England had a sustainable development unit which in 2010, for example, produced a document called Procuring for Carbon Reduction. However, the relentless and short-sighted political pressure for cost savings from hostile governments means that its activities around purchasing have been significantly marginalised since then.

5.4 Ethical procurement by local authorities and public bodies is commonly circumscribed by legal rules

One of the attractive features about ethical purchasing as a campaign tool is that it's almost impossible for people opposed to its views to stop it happening. For most ethical purchasers – companies, individuals, and NGOs – they are free to spend more on a less damaging product or service if that's what they want to do. Ethical procurement by local authorities is the one exception to this feature and there is much evidence of national governments trying to prevent it happening.

Some of this was a result of good faith interventions to try to stop corruption. Local governance structures and large budgets have been a temptation for greedy local politicians and local businesses throughout the ages. If you force local buyers to procure only on price, then at least people served by the authority are not losing significant sums of money even if friends of the politicians are winning contracts.

However, many attempts to suppress ethical purchasing occur because the political party in control of a national government is different to the political party in control of a local authority. Margaret Thatcher's Local Government Act of 1988, for example, specifically banned purchasing which addressed issues such as labour rights and country of origin of business interests (specifically trying to stop support for the South Africa boycott campaign to oppose institutionalised racism). And the tender regime implied by the Swedish Law on Public Procurements also prevents authorities from considering social factors.

Regulatory restrictions in this space have encouraged less ethical corporations to choose to challenge local authorities in court rather than improve their behaviour. In the Netherlands, for example, a coffee company challenged one local authority in the courts because they had a fair trade tea and coffee policy. This was later reformed by a clarifying ruling by the EU.

And in the USA in 1996, a group of corporations sued the state of Massachusetts over its law preventing public authorities from purchasing from companies operating in Burma, which was at that time ruled by an oppressive military regime. The US Supreme Court ruled that the State's rules were illegal.

These legal restrictions and challenges have created an atmosphere of uncertainty in many local authorities, and officials have been known to advise wrongly that ethical purchasing is not possible. Some of the more developed campaigns, Fairtrade towns in particular, provide detailed legal advice for local authorities on how to word procurement contracts and policies to remain within the law.

Fortunately, in Europe in particular, the benefits of ethical procurement have led to clarifying laws which encourage it to take place particularly around consensual issues like sustainability. In some cases, the even more effective approach of requiring local authorities to purchase in this way has been adopted (see Chapter 6). However in some key areas, such as allowing local authorities to consider tax conduct, the law is still, unfathomably, a barrier to campaigns for common sense and widely supported reforms.

5.5 Like any organisation, stakeholder surveys or a democratic mandate can give useful legitimacy to ethical purchasing programmes

The first principle of ethical purchasing in 1.1.2 contains the statement "what is ethical isn't always agreed by everyone." And for all organisations, a common principle derived from this is that it makes sense to seek broad support amongst stakeholders for ethical purchasing programmes.

For democratically elected public authorities, this is relatively easy as they are already designed to give a formal public voice to local decision-making. Political parties of most colours have included promises to encourage sustainable purchasing in their manifestos for many years now and the adoption of ethical purchasing policies are commonly preceded by voting on a resolution or bill in a democratically elected chamber. The Massachusetts Burma Law mentioned in 5.4 is just one example of where this process occurred. And the Fairtrade towns' campaign, also mentioned above, provides an example of a developed campaign which provides 'model resolutions' for towns wanting to support the campaign to adopt.

And as we have also seen in this chapter, political difference between local authorities and national governments have been known to create tension around what ethical issues may be considered. However, having a democratic local mandate for ethical purchasing, even for more controversial ethical issues, can make government attempts to suppress it look particularly malign. For example, the UK Conservative government's attempt in 2016 to prevent Local Authorities from supporting the Israel Boycott Divestment and Sanctions campaign promoted by Palestinian solidarity groups was opposed even by members of its own political party. The government ruling in this case was later rejected as unlawful by the High Court in 2017 following a judicial review.

For public purchasers which are not directly elected, consultations with stakeholders around ethical purchasing programmes will be similar to those discussed for smaller companies and Civil Society Organisations in Section 7.1.2.

5.6 Like all ethical purchasing, working collectively with other groups will give the greatest impact

This general principle only applies to some local authority purchasing. In some cases, the local authority will be many times larger than a local contractor or supplier it will be using, and it will be able to specify, for example, "that all the workers wear kilts" (or are unionised) if it wishes (1.5.2).

In other cases, perhaps where the supplier is a multinational company or where the local authority purchase is only for a relatively small value, it may be less easy to specify particular ethical criteria in contracts. This means that to have greater impact, an authority could explore working with others – like most other types of purchasers need to do.

For some more developed campaigns, there are already groups of local authorities acting collectively around popular issues. We discussed above, for example, how the Fairtrade town movement (5.4) and the carbon divestment movement (5.25) were working specifically with groups of local authorities to achieve their goals.

On sustainable purchasing, there are a number of networks, including the Local Governments for Sustainability ICLEI (originally standing for the International Council for Local Environmental Initiatives). It is a global network of more than 1,500 cities, towns, and regions 'committed to sustainability' and which includes procurement amongst its specialities.

Working collectively can also reduce (by sharing) the costs of research to help understand and identify ethical issues and ethical suppliers in supply chains.

5.7 Like all ethical purchasing, communicating a programme with stakeholders and suppliers will give it the greatest impact

This is another general principle which applies across all ethical purchasing (1.8). Anecdotally, the legal uncertainty around more innovative ethical purchasing ideas at local authorities can mean that they may be carried out without a blaze of publicity. The downside to this approach is that the impact of the policy could well be lower. If a local authority requires contractors to have equal opportunity or environmental policies, for example, all the businesses in the region which would like to be contractors will adopt these policies, not just the ones currently contracting.

There are three main ways stakeholder communication is usually manifested by local authorities.

(a)   *In tender documents*

It is now very common for tender documents to require an equal opportunities policy at supplier companies, both in the UK and elsewhere. Lewisham council, for example, provides an 18-page guidance document for suppliers on this sustainability issues, and most UK councils in 2018 used an agreed framework called the West Midlands Forum's 'Common Standard'.

Other requirements, such as for an environmental policy, may appear in tender documents too.

(b)   *In supplier questionnaires*

Even before ethical issues are considered, most local authorities will have a supplier database populated with information from supplier questionnaires. It is not complex to add additional questions on ethical issues relating to a product, company, or employment conditions, for example.

(c)   *Less formally in council resolutions or in policy documents or on websites*

As mentioned in Section 5.4, it is common for purchasing campaigns to prepare draft resolutions for local authorities to adopt and materials to help them communicate a decision. The Fairtrade towns and carbon divestment movement campaigns were the examples used, and both have worked in this space.

5.8 Running ethical purchasing programmes in large organisations can lead to complex bureaucracies

In Section 6.3.1, it is noted how the US Department of Defense once had 500 staff to monitor its social compliance programmes. Often a systematic approach to a problem is good. An organisation can look at what its biggest spending areas are in order to maximise impact at the beginning of a programme. It can develop questionnaires, databases, and approved lists of suppliers. There are many good resources on sustainable procurement for complex bureaucracies, such as those produced by the Chartered Institute of Purchasing and Supply in the UK.

However, a lack of political direction or political will can see such programmes drift and lose bite over time if not frequently reviewed. Some research in this area has shown that while the majority of UK local authorities had some environmental procurement rules by the beginning of the 21st century, many programmes lacked effectiveness.

Trying to regularly measure and communicate the impact of such pro-grammes is a good way to keep stakeholders encouraged that the whole operation has a point.

5.9 Some local authorities have developed supplier seminars and even created their own ethical suppliers

It is not uncommon for local authorities to find that smaller, more ethical companies are not tendering or even able to tender for local contracts. So, just as larger companies with environmental or social goals may need to work with smaller suppliers to help them develop towards these goals (see 4.9.2), local authorities can work to encourage different supplier types to bid. The bureaucratisation of purchasing, discussed above, can be a bar-rier to smaller companies, and so some regions have provided training, or seminars, or other materials in order to try to encourage these types of firms to bid for contracts. Other approaches, such as breaking contracts down into smaller parcels, have also been successful. There is a fair amount of literature in this space providing more detail here.

Just as campaigners looking for an ethical business to drive consumers towards have sometimes had to set up these businesses themselves (e.g. Fairphone), local authorities concerned with social issues of economic development can also set up businesses designed to supply them with par-ticular services. Preston, mentioned above, is trying to set up worker co-ops in IT and food to do just this. The inspiration for this approach came from Cleveland, Ohio, where the worker-owned Evergreen Cooperatives was set up in 2008 to collaborate with the city government and the local Cleveland Foundation. A contract laundry, an urban farm, and an energy business have all been set up as co-operatives to serve the city. This approach is now referred to as the Cleveland model.

5.10 Some governments are beginning to require that local authorities begin to purchase ethically

If, as discussed in Section 10.7.2, all purchases have a political element, by having no policy local authorities may be actually undermining some of their social or environmental goals.

Going beyond permitting ethical procurement to happen and requir-ing all public sector purchasers to address collectively shared issues like sustainability and social welfare is also as an action that governments (which share such goals) should rationally take.

Legislation is apparently evolving in some countries (such as Belgium and Finland) to require social clauses in public tenders.

As discussed below, ideal policies should address sustainability, social welfare, assets/investments, and solidarity. They should look to work collectively with other groups and also have regular (at least annual) impact reviews to maintain effectiveness. But they also should be publicly communicated and democratically controlled. Variety in local ethical responses to current issues is not undesirable. A diverse ecosystem of approaches is, after all, most likely to generate proven effective models that others can then share.

References and notes

5.1   Public procurement as percentage of GDP. See e.g. https://ec.europa.eu/growth/single-market/public-procurement_en

5.2.1 South Africa solidarity purchasing; https://www.aamarchives.org/who-was-involved/local-authorities.html, and Richard Knight (1990) *Sanctions, Disinvestment, and US.* Corporations in South Africa, in Sanctioning Apartheid. Africa World Press.

5.2.2 NEF and Northumberland Council. www.theguardian.com/society/2005/mar/30/guardiansocietysupplement5

Preston; www.theguardian.com/commentisfree/2018/jan/31/preston-hit-rock-bottom-took-back-control

Tax avoidance; https://fairtaxmark.net/sourced-campaign/

5.2.3 H. Walker and S. Brammer, S (2012) The relationship between sustainable procurement and e-procurement in the public sector. *International Journal of Production Economics* 140(1), pp. 256–268. November 2012.

DEFRA UK (2006) Procuring the Future: Sustainable Procurement National Action Plan: Recommendations from the Sustainable Procurement Task Force. Also contains information about Japan and the Energy Star label in the USA.

5.2.4 Social enterprise in Europe: At the crossroads of market, public policies, and third sector,

Jacques Defourny and Marthe Nyssens in Policy and Society Volume 29, 2010. Issue 3: Financing the Third Sector

5.2.5 Divestment during the Anti-Apartheid campaign is well documented. See e.g. Kinloch Massie, Robert (1997) Loosing the Bands. The United States and South Africa in the Apartheid Years.

At the time of writing, gofossilfree.org was a live campaign with detailed information on its website.

Preston again; www.theguardian.com/cities/2017/apr/11/preston-cleveland-model-lessons-recovery-rust-belt

5.3 (b) Klein, Naomi (1999) No Logo. Many universities also have sustainable procurement programmes. See e.g. www.ed.ac.uk/sustainability/what-we-do/supply-chains/initiatives/fairness-trade-sustainable-procurement

(c) See e.g. www.sduhealth.org.uk/areas-of-focus/commissioning-and-procurement/procurement.aspx

5.4 On the Local Government Act, see Local Council and Ethical Buying: Ethical Consumer Magazine, October and November 1991.

On the Netherlands Fairtrade coffee case, see e.g. https://europeanlawblog.eu/2012/05/11/fair-trade-coffee-and-tea-under-the-procurement-directive/

On the Massachusetts Burma Law, see e.g. www.nytimes.com/2000/06/20/us/supreme-court-foreign-policy-issue-justices-overturn-state-law-myanmar.html

Public Procurement for Fairtrade Towns (2014) A guide for Fairtrade campaigners to influence public spending in favour of disadvantaged farmers and workers in the developing world. At www.fairtrade.org.uk/get%20involved//In-your-community/Towns/Public-Procurement/Resources-and-Useful-Links

5.5 BDS in the UK; https://bdsmovement.net/news/uk-high-court-rules-favour-local-councils-who-support-boycott-israeli-occupation

5.6 For International Council for Local Environmental Initiatives, see www.iclei.org

5.7 Lewisham (2012) Sustainable Procurement Code of Practice for all organisations who wish to contract with the Council

West Midlands Forum, see e.g. Craig, Ronald L. (2007) Systemic Discrimination in Employment and the Promotion of Ethnic Equality. Brill, Netherlands. At page 218.

5.8 CIPS (May 2009) Sustainable Procurement. Knowledge Summary. Chartered Institute of Purchasing and Supply. UK.

H. Walker and S. Brammer (2007) 'Sustainable procurement in the United Kingdom public sector.' Bath, U. K.

H. Walker and S. Brammer (2011) Sustainable procurement in the public sector: An international comparative study. *International Journal of Operations.*

5.9 Training suppliers. See e.g. CLES Bulletin No.22 (May2004) Local Government Procurement, Social Enterprise and the Third Sector
For Preston and Cleveland, see 5.2.5.

5.10 Schulten, Alsos, Burgess, and Pedersen (2012) Pay and other social clauses in European public procurement: An overview on regulation and practices with a focus on Denmark, Germany, Norway, Switzerland, and the United Kingdom at www.boeckler.de/pdf/wsi_schulten_pay_and_ other_social_causes.pdf

6

ETHICAL PURCHASING AND THE ROLE OF GOVERNMENTS

6.1 Governments can not only address ethical issues in their own buying but they can also choose to facilitate it elsewhere

Because governments have some control over the economic framework within which ethical purchasing occurs, principles for governments are slightly more complex than for those of other institutions. In brief:

(a) Governments can make sure their own purchasing follows ethical principles; and
(b) Governments can also choose to encourage ethical purchasing in wider society by requiring transparency at producers, or by providing training, resources, or other incentives to help it to occur.

We explore these two main areas in detail in this chapter.

Finally, it is noted that regulation can often be a better solution to some of the problems that many civil society ethical purchasing campaigns are trying to address.

DOI: 10.4324/9781003200185-6

In Section 5.5, the principle was stated that "surveying stakeholders or a democratic mandate gives legitimacy to ethical purchasing programmes," and the way that elected governments already have a framework for this kind of legitimacy was discussed in more detail.

6.1.1 Governments may be targeted by campaigners around their purchasing in the same way as other big institutions

A classic case in the UK occurred in 2002, when around 100 Greenpeace protesters staged a protest at a government building in Whitehall, which was being refurbished for the Cabinet Office. They were drawing attention to the use of endangered African rainforest wood to make doors and windows and some people stood outside with placards and banners bearing the slogan 'ancient forest crime zone'. Others, who entered the building to replace the doors with sustainable alternatives, were arrested. The government had made a pledge to use only legal and sustainable materials during the renovation work.

The protest prompted an all-party committee of MPs to investigate the general pledge to buy sustainable timber and branded it 'an absolute failure' in a detailed report issued in July of that year (see Section 6.5).

6.2 There are five reasons why it makes sense for governments to purchase ethically and to promote its wider practice

a) It is likely to be economically inefficient for society to absorb social and environmental costs after the event. For example, it may be better for public sector organisations to buy exclusively renewable energy now rather than pay for the costs of addressing flood damage later on. Section 10.2.2, 'Theoretical principles', explores in more detail the idea that societies can function both more efficiently and more humanely when ethical purchasing is widely practised.

b) Powerful institutions with large procurement budgets can persuade supplier companies to address ethical issues very quickly.

c) Research carried out by governments on which products, processes, or companies to favour can be placed in the public domain to inform consumers and private sector buyers.

d) Government purchasing can stimulate markets and lower prices for innovative ethical and environmental products like solar cells or alternative fuels.

e)   The general public will ignore any government attempts to encourage responsible purchasing more widely if it is clear that governments are not themselves already acting on their own advice.

6.3 Ethical procurement by governments can be demonstrably effective and can be broken down into four main types

6.3.1 Social procurement

In the 1950s, the idea of using public purchasing power to promote wider social objectives became increasingly commonplace in the USA. Firms seeking government contracts were, for example, required to comply with requirements not to discriminate against women or minorities and to correct existing imbalances. Strangely enough, the otherwise ethically challenged US Department of Defense apparently had a staff of more than 500 people to monitor social compliance at supplier companies at the time, and research showed that it was very effective at increasing demand for black workers.

Promoting equal opportunities and diversity at suppliers through procurement is now common across developed Western economies.

6.3.2 Sustainable procurement

Many sustainable procurement programmes are clearly effective too, and are now becoming widespread. In 2003, the European Commission, in its snappily titled 'Communication on Integrated Product Policy', encouraged Member States to draw up publicly available National Action Plans (NAPs) for greening their public procurement. By May 2017, the following 23 countries had NAPs: Austria, Belgium, Bulgaria, Croatia, Cyprus, Czech Republic, Denmark, Finland, France, Germany, Ireland, Italy, Latvia, Lithuania, Malta, Netherlands, Poland, Portugal, Slovakia, Slovenia, Spain, Sweden, and a pre-Brexit UK.

Others have been better at communicating actual programme impacts. The Japanese Ministry of the Environment, for example, estimated that its green purchasing programme had led to a reduction in greenhouse gas emissions of 210,787 tonnes of CO_2 equivalent in 2013. This is, perhaps disappointingly, about 120th of the annual emissions of an average coal-fired power plant in the USA.

The idea of sustainable procurement has also spread beyond Western economies. In Brazil, in the first nine months of 2012, for example, the government claimed that sustainable purchases and contracts had increased by 194% with £8.5 million being spent on goods and services using sustainable criteria (computers 39%, paper 16.4%, air conditioning 15.7%). And in Chile, Chile Compra, the body responsible for managing procurement there, claimed that 27% of its purchases had sustainability criteria.

6.3.3 Buying from national producers

In Section 5.2.2, the idea of local authorities buying locally in order to boost local economies was discussed. This same principle can be observed being practised by governments throughout history. Governments would 'work closely with' companies which were national champions, or which they partially or wholly owned, or which provided employment in economically depressed areas, or which were in strategically important industries ('defence'), from which it would make sense for them to buy from.

However, in the same way that local authority procurement is often circumscribed by rules set by national governments, this kind of nationalistic procurement has become less prevalent in recent decades as international treaties on trade have tried to restrict its use (see 10.1.4).

6.3.4 Solidarity purchasing, political purchasing, and sanctions

Economic sanctions, which are an enforced boycott of trade with a particular country, have been practised by governments throughout history. Only loosely connected to ethics at best, they are more often motivated by geopolitical or strategic national self-interest. They have been operated by the USA against Cuba, Iran, and Russia amongst others, by Arab states against Israel, and by a variety of governments – in a more ostensibly ethical way – against Apartheid South Africa.

In 1932, John Foster Dulles, who became an American Secretary of State, wrote in 'Boycotts and Peace' that "The great advantage of economic sanctions is that on the one had they can be very potent, while on the other hand, they do not involve that resort to force which is repugnant to our objective of peace." N. Craig Smith, amongst other writers, has explored the idea that avoiding the use of force is, in itself, an ethical goal. When collectively imposed, through the UN's international legal frameworks, the likelihood of ethical motivations is higher.

The opposite of sanctions could be termed solidarity purchasing and has also been observed being practised by Local Authorities (5.2.1) as well as governments. Russia, for example, chose to buy Cuban produce to support a fellow communist state during the US boycott, and there are very many other similar examples.

It is clear though that sanctions and solidarity purchasing could be more comfortably viewed as a form of political purchasing (see Section 10.5.3) than ethical purchasing.

6.4 Governments can also research into ethical performance for their own purchasing and share the results

As mentioned in Chapter 10, markets operate 'imperfectly' without perfect information. Using rational criteria to choose one ethical product or supplier over another can be highly complex (see e.g. Section 2.6). Governments can pool resources centrally to undertake detailed research of the type that might be able to provide answers.

The EU has developed Green Public Procurement criteria for a whole range of products such as computers, paper, food, and electricity, and publishes this on a website. The US government has also generated programmes such as Electronic Product Environmental Assessment Tool and Energy Star labelling, and consolidates information for federal buyers on a Green Procurement Compilation website.

Unfortunately, corporate lobbying of governments on a wide range of issues (10.1.3) is already a well-recognised phenomenon, and pressure to keep the bar low in such projects is not uncommon. In the UK, for example, there was a 'central point of expertise on timber' which published data for all its departments on a website about the various sustainable timber labelling schemes, options, and rules. It could have been more strongly supportive of the higher labelling standards (it inexplicably gave FCS and Programme for the Endorsement of Forest Certification equal weight; see Chapter 8). It was finally 'cut' in 2016, giving the impression that austerity (or low taxation) was more important than sustainability.

Nevertheless, these centrally funded 'buyers guides' can also be useful for other non-governmental groups, which is why their appearance in the public domain is important.

6.5 Some ethical procurement by governments has been criticised for being bureaucratic and ineffective

Like any political project, government attempts to make improvements may not always be successful and may rightly be criticised as such. In the UK, a Parliamentary committee looking at green procurement practices in 2002, for example, stated that "ministers seemed to have indulged in saying all the right things but have done nothing about it ... We have been unable to find any evidence of a systematic change in the pattern of public timber procurement" (see also Section 6.1.1).

For such interventions to have genuine impact, it would seem obvious that they need at least two additional elements:

(a) Ethical purchasing should be requirement of government departments rather than simply a power; and
(b) There should be annual public reporting of the impact of ethical procurement schemes so that all parties can get a clear sense of progress or indeed the lack of progress if this is the case.

6.6 Intervening in the market to facilitate ethical purchasing can be very effective

6.6.1 Governments can improve the flow of information on ethical issues

Drawing heavily on Ethical Consumer Research Association's original 2001 Manifesto, it is possible to observe that consumers and other purchasers are hampered in their ability to purchase ethically by the lack of information on which to base decisions. There are four main areas where governments can act to help improve the flow of information: labelling, disclosure, publishing, and the regulation of ethical claims.

In an ideal world, a government could systematically review each of these areas to see what else it might do to enable more socially aware economic behaviour.

(a)   *Labelling*

Compulsory labelling around ethical issues has proved to be one of the most effective interventions that governments can make. For example, the European A-G energy labelling scheme was recognised as so effective that it was copied in a number of other countries. Although providing information on the energy efficiency of a product can allow people to reduce running costs, for many it also allows consumers to make a less energy intensive choice for ethical reasons.

European regulators have also required consumer product labels for some environmentally controversial ingredients such as genetically modified foods and palm oil. Country of origin labelling can also be useful for buyers wanting to practice solidarity purchasing or boycotts, though this was not always the intention of this label.

Ethical Consumer argues that disclosure of a product's constituents, as is required in the case of foodstuff, should be extended to all other products to facilitate a much wider range of possible ethical decision-making. This kind of radical transparency is already being practised by some firms seeking to tell a feel-good story about their own product's origins (see Section 4.7).

(b)   *Disclosure*

Different jurisdictions have different rules over what companies must disclose, although there is a general trend to require more information on ethical issues and impacts with most progress perhaps being made in France. Since 2013, all companies with over 500 employees are required to issue an annual social and environmental report. Companies must provide information in 42 areas, including: employment, labour relations, health and safety, pollution, waste management, energy consumption, social impacts, relations with stakeholders, and human rights (see Appendix A2). Importantly, these reports are subject to verification by an independent third party. This allows clear benchmarking by a whole range of purchasers and investors and by companies themselves.

Requiring disclosure of financial assets is also a good way to encourage ethical scrutiny of the activities of banks and investment firms. In the USA, for example, but not anywhere else, mutual funds must disclose their holdings regularly to the regulator.

Finally, there has been a growing requirement on companies to disclose policies on controversial issues. The 2015 Modern Slavery Act in the UK, for example, influenced by a 2010 regulation in California, required companies to disclose what, if anything, they were doing to try to prevent slavery in their supply chains.

Finally, with the current fashion for outsourcing government functions to private companies, it can be argued that freedom of information rules should apply to companies performing such roles if the role of democracy is not to be curtailed.

(c)   Publishing

Governments can choose to publish information on company performance against social and environmental issues. The US Toxics Release Inventory is perhaps the classic example of this kind of intervention. Formed in 1986, it provides a web-accessible database, placing in the public domain all toxic chemical emissions 'consents', releases, and enforcement data. It has now been copied, to some degree, in at least 50 other countries.

It can be even more useful for ethical purchasers if governments choose to interpret the data and to produce league tables or 'name and shame' the worst performers. Companies obviously hate this and fight hard to prevent it happening, which it why it is seen less often. The Labour government in the UK in 1999 published a list of the worst polluters, pointing out that it already published performance league tables for public sector institutions (schools), so it seemed reasonable to do the same for private sector ones too in an effort to improve performance. We also discussed the Global Benchmarking Alliance in 3.5.7. This is an international collaboration ranking multinational companies on human rights which involves governments and other actors.

(d)   Regulation of ethical claims

The rise of ethical purchasing has not been helped by companies making false, misleading, or just plain bizarre ethical claims about their products. Volkswagen's advertising of environmentally friendly diesel cars in the USA is just one example, although it did lead to a particularly high profile $4.3 billion settlement. Many advertising regulators have however struggled with ethical claims, which are sometimes complex to evidence, and so can be useful to set up systems to address them directly.

In 2005, the Nordic Consumer Ombudsmen (Finland, Denmark, Norway, and Sweden) adopted a joint guideline on *Ethical and Environmental Marketing Claims*, which extended previous rules on environmental advertising to include social and ethical issues such as child labour and working conditions.

The EU has also long enforced rules for the labelling and promotion of both imported and regionally produced organic foods, which have been incredibly important in maintaining the integrity of the movement.

6.6.2 Formal education in ethical buying is critical too

Socially responsible consumption, and its history and diversity, should be required learning across all schools. Young people are entering the market as purchasers at ever earlier ages, and unless it is taught, there may be no reason for young people to suspect that unlimited consumption or unethical consumption of any kind is problematic. According to an Organisation for Economic Co-operation and Development (OECD) report in 2008, sustainable consumption had already become part of the formal curricula across many Western countries by that time. Measuring energy consumption, waste recycling and water use appeared to be common elements. Learning about, for example, fair trade or problems with human rights in clothing supply chains appears to be less common, but equally important.

In the UK, during the Labour government of Tony Blair in 2002, the idea of citizenship education was introduced across all schools. In 2004, consumer rights and responsibilities and fair trade were incorporated into teaching citizenship for 14-year-olds, though it became marginalised under later Conservative administrations.

A study from 2016 in China has revealed that the government there has undertaken eco-awareness campaigns for citizens there to create 'an environmentally-friendly and resource-conserving society'.

6.6.3 Governments can also require local authorities and other public purchasers to procure ethically in specific areas

This idea was discussed in more detail in Section 5.10.

6.7 Incentivising ethical purchasing through tax or fiscal arrangements is also an effective tool which governments can use

As we discuss at 10.1, sometimes ethical products are 'internalising social costs' often 'externalised' by other producers. This can make the cost of some ethical products higher. As we have also seen in Chapter 9, most data suggest that the majority of consumers will not pay huge extra costs for ethical choices, and therefore subsidy may be important in some markets where high take-up is important.

The most common examples in the early 21st century have been subsidies to encourage the purchase of electric cars or other vehicles, which can be two or three times the price of ordinary cars. Most major economies now have subsidies of some kind, ranging from large cash grants in Norway to reduce the purchase price to that of an equivalent gas-guzzling brand, to small reductions in value-added tax (VAT) or road taxes as seen in, for example, Greece. In China, the subsidies are paid direct to the manufacturers; however, all these interventions still rely on motivated consumers to create impact.

Similar subsidies, often in the form of a guaranteed price for electricity generated, have emerged for consumers fitting solar panels to the roofs of their houses. And in Europe, there is a power for governments to set lower rates of VAT (purchase tax) for a wide range of energy-saving items like insulation and ground source heat pumps.

It seems though that this area of government intervention generally is underdeveloped and has not really kept up with a market now awash with ethical products. Reduction of VAT on Fairtrade products by northern governments, for example, could (notionally at least) come from overseas aid budgets and address some of the root causes of global inequalities. But the wider use of purchase tax to make cost-internalising producers price competitive seems like a no-brainer.

Similar interventions around ethical investment could also be better developed. In the UK, we have had 'social investment tax relief' for some years to encourage investment in social enterprises. And, Ethical Consumer in its manifesto suggests that certain company forms, such as not-for-profits or B-corporations, could receive favourable tax rates to encourage their formation.

6.8 Governments can also support multi-stakeholder initiatives

A multi-stakeholder initiative (MSI) in the ethical purchasing space usually involves companies and campaigners (and sometimes other stakeholders) getting together to try to solve a particular problem collaboratively. Many, but not all, MSIs sit behind the ethical labelling schemes, which we discuss in Chapter 8.

The classic case of a UK-based MSI supported by government is the UK's Ethical Trading Initiative (ETI), which was discussed in 4.4.3.

In the USA, a similar initiative created by Bill Clinton in 1996 led to the creation of the Fair Labour Association (FLA). Unlike the ETI, which does not endorse products or companies, the FLA audits company supply chains and therefore endorses some companies. This has led to trades unions refusing to join the initiative and for it being criticised for particular endorsements, most notably of the giant Chinese factory Foxxcon supplying Apple's Iphones. The FLA is now an independent not-for-profit organisation.

6.8.1 Clarifying anti-trust laws

Sometimes when companies try to collaborate to address sustainability and social justice issues, these can appear to fall foul of 'anti-trust' laws in some jurisdictions. Anti-trust laws were designed, quite rightly, to stop companies agreeing to keep prices high to cheat purchasers. As we discuss in more detail in 10.2.3, governments need to clarify – with some urgency – that for genuine programmes (perhaps assessed using some of the possible metrics discussed in Chapter 8), these rules will not apply.

6.9 Regulatory solutions to the problem of externalising social and environmental costs remain important

As noted in 6.1, regulation can often be a better solution to some of the problems that many civil society ethical purchasing campaigns are trying to address.

6.9.1 Solutions directly affecting consumer markets

'Choice editing' is a term currently favoured for removing unhelpful products from the market. Banning unethical products is another way of saying the same thing. When the link between chlorofluorocarbons (CFCs) in aerosol cans and ozone depletion in the upper atmosphere became known in the 1980s, governments around the world reacted differently. In the USA, following consumer campaigning, there was a ban. In the UK, with a free market idealist at the government helm, it required consumers' boycotts to persuade manufacturers to 'voluntarily' withdraw these products from the market. This example is quite illustrative of how civil society campaigns can step in when the obvious regulatory solutions are somehow failing to arrive. As we can see in Section 6.9.4, there was eventually a ground-breaking international treaty developed to 'edit' this choice from consumer markets globally.

It is also worth noting that within the EU energy labelling scheme, there is also a programme to progressively remove the worst performing products (E to G) from many of the markets it works in (e.g. fridges).

6.9.2 Solutions directly addressing consumer concerns through regulating producers

The tendency for competitive markets to reward the cheaper products that unethical behaviours can bring has been responsible for much of the growth in the movement for ethical purchasing that this book is charting. The most obvious solution in many cases is simply to regulate to prevent the problems from occurring or the market from operating in this way. Banning a particular type of product (e.g. eggs from hens in battery cages) has already been discussed under choice editing above; however, governments can also address concerns through direct controls on producers. These might ban inputs (like some pesticides) or require outputs like emissions to water to be treated in a certain way. They can also, in a kind of reverse of choice editing, enforce minimum standards across a sector, such as the minimum energy efficiency requirements found in housebuilding regulations in many countries in the 21st century.

Another theme in this book though is that it can be difficult for governments to regulate in supply chains that stretch into other countries. The ideal solution to this can be to collaborate at an international level, which is covered in 6.9.4.

6.9.3 Solutions addressing corporate power

More rarely, governments may wish to try to address corporate power imbalances, which lie at the heart of some regulatory failure. Much has been written about how corporate lobbyists can 'capture' government departments (10.1.3), and their influence has been palpable at key moments in history, such as during international climate change negotiations. One approach has been to require transparency so that people can see what it going on, and some lobbying activities or expenditures now have to be declared to a limited extent in the USA and Europe. This is a complex area and beyond the scope of this book.

6.9.4 *Solutions at an international level*

We have noted how one key driver of the growth of ethical purchasing has been the absence of effective regulation across some global supply chains to prohibit unethical activities (such as child labour) from taking place. There are limits to what individual countries can do and it is clear that more international regulatory collaboration could solve many of these problems effectively. Many books have been written about why this doesn't happen and how it could. Again, it is beyond the scope of this book to discuss this further.

There is one poster child, however, for this kind of international collaboration which shows what can happen when the political will exists – and perhaps where the vested commercial interested are relatively small. The 'Montreal Protocol on substances that deplete the ozone layer' was agreed in 1987 and is now ratified by all 196 states and the EU. It was also lauded for the speed with which it was created and adopted with 'only' 14 years elapsing between the scientific research discovery (1973) and the international solution. A number of reports have been written about how difficult subsequent enforcement has been, with criminal gangs becoming involved in the illegal trade in CFCs; but the treaty itself is generally an example of what can be done and a cause for hope for what could be done elsewhere.

The idea of effective democratic global governance is also discussed in 10.6.4.

References and notes

6.1.1 BBC website Wednesday, 10 April, 2002. Green protesters arrested in Whitehall
http://news.bbc.co.uk/1/hi/uk_politics/1920905.stm
UK Government Environmental Audit Committee (2002) *Buying Time for Forests: Timber and Public Procurement*, July 2002, HC 792-I. https://publications.parliament.uk/pa/cm200203/cmselect/cmenvaud/909/909.pdf

6.3.1 US Department of Defence: Local Council and Ethical Buying: Ethical Consumer Magazine, October and November 1991
Equality and Human Rights Commission (2013) Buying better outcomes: Mainstreaming equality considerations in procurement: A guide for public authorities in England. https://www.equalityhumanrights.com/sites/default/files/buying_better_outcomes_final.pdf

6.3.2 For more information on Europe's sustainable procurement action plans, see https://ec.europa.eu/environment/gpp/action_plan_en.htm

Ministry of Environment, Japan (2016) Introduction to Green Purchasing Legislation in Japan. www.env.go.jp/policy/hozen/green/kokusai_platform/2015report/handbook_eng.pdf

For US power plant emissions, see e.g: https://www.eurekalert.org/pub_releases/2007-11/cfgd-crc111207.php

https://assets.publishing.service.gov.uk/government/uploads/system/uploads/attachment_data/file/69417/pb11710-procuring-the-future-060607.pdf

For Brazil and Chile, see Ethical Consumer Magazine Issue 142. June 2013. p. 32

6.3.3 For more information on national procurement and the WTO's role in trying to manage it, see e.g. https://www.globaltrademag.com/erasing-the-global-gains-from-the-wto-government-procurement-agreement/

6.3.4 There are whole chapters in this subject in: N. Craig Smith (1990) *Morality and the Market*. Routledge. London.

6.4 For EU Green Public Procurement criteria, see https://ec.europa.eu/environment/gpp/eu_gpp_criteria_en.htm

The US Green Procurement Compilation website is a "comprehensive green purchasing resource designed for federal contracting personnel and program managers" and can be found at: https://sftool.gov/greenprocurement

More details on the UK Central Point for Expertise on Timber are available from: www.gov.uk/government/collections/cpet-resources-for-government-procurers-suppliers-and-businesses

6.5 Guardian 2002, Government is a green failure, say MPs; www.theguardian.com/politics/2002/jul/24/greenpolitics.uk

6.6 Ethical Consumer 2001 Manifesto; www.ethicalconsumer.org/sites/default/files/inline-files/Manifesto%202001_0.pdf

(a) OECD (2008) *Promoting Sustainable Consumption: Good Practices in OECD Countries* (PDF has a chapter on standards and mandatory labels).

For more on EU palm oil and food labelling, see www.theguardian.com/sustainable-business/2014/dec/12/eu-labelling-changes-palm-oil-consumer-change

(b) For compulsory corporate reporting requirements, see e.g. Annual Report on the OECD Guidelines for Multinational Enterprises 2013. Responsible Business Conduct in Action:

US SEC reporting requirements; www.investopedia.com/ask/answers/ 091715/how-often-do-mutual-funds-report-their-holdings.asp

Modern Slavery; www.theguardian.com/sustainable-business/2015/ dec/14/modern-slavery-act-explained-business-responsibility-supply-chain

(c) Toxics release inventories; see www.epa.gov/toxics-release-inventory-tri-program/tri-around-world

ENDS Report (June 2000); https://www.endsreport.com/article/ 1557966/agency-tempers-hall-shame-pollution-leagues

(d) BBC News Website (29 March 2016) FTC sues Volkswagen over diesel car advertisements. https://www.bbc.co.uk/news/business-35918792

OECD (2008) *Promoting Sustainable Consumption: Good Practices in OECD Countries* (PDF has a chapter on advertising too which talks about the Nordic consumer ombudsman as well as organic labelling).

6.6.2 OECD (2008) *Promoting Sustainable Consumption: Good Practices in OECD Countries.*

J. Pykett, P. Cloke, C. Barnett, N. Clarke and A. Malpass (2010) Learning to be global citizens: The rationalities of fair-trade education. *Environment and Planning D: Society and Space,* 28(3), pp. 487–508.

Placing 'sustainability' in context: Narratives of sustainable consumption in Nanjing, China. Chen Liu, Gill Valentine, Robert M. Vanderbeck, Katie McQuaid and Kristina Diprose. February 2018: *Journal of Social and Cultural Geography.*

6.7 Electric car subsidies; www.volkswagenag.com/en/news/ stories/2019/05/how-electric-car-incentives-around-the-world-work. html – Motavalli, Jim (2010–06-02). China to start pilot program, providing subsidies for electric cars and hybrids. *New York Times.* Retrieved 2010–06-02, https://www.acea.be/publications/article/ overview-of-incentives-for-buying-electric-vehicles

Solar panel subsidy schemes; www.theguardian.com/environment/2018/ jul/19/subsidies-for-new-household-solar-panels-to-end-next-year

European Commission, DG Environment (2008) The use of differential VAT rates to promote changes in consumption and innovation Final report. https://ec.europa.eu/environment/enveco/taxation/pdf/vat_final.pdf

Social investment tax relief; www.centreforpublicimpact.org/ case-study/social-investment-tax-relief-scheme-united-kingdom/

Ethical Consumer 2001 manifesto; www.ethicalconsumer.org/sites/ default/files/inline-files/Manifesto%202001.pdf

6.8   Fair Labor Association in the USA; www.fairlabor.org/about-us; and www. nytimes.com/2012/02/17/business/early-praise-in-foxconn-inspection-brings-doubt.html?_r=1

6.9.1 Choice editing; see e.g. UK Sustainable Development Commission (May 2006)

Looking Back, Looking Forward: Lessons in Choice Editing for Sustainability.

CFCs: Social Learning Group (2001) Learning to Manage Global Environmental Risks - Politics, Science, and the Environment, at p. 96 for the FoE boycott.

David Vogel (2012) *The Politics of Precaution: Regulating Health, Safety, and Environmental Risks in Europe and the United States.* Princeton University Press. Princeton at p122 for the US boycott etc.

Exploring the relationship between environmental regulation and competitiveness: A case study on the *Energy Labelling* Directive. Final Report for DEFRA 2007.

6.9.2 UNITED NATIONS ECONOMIC COMMISSION FOR EUROPE Joint Task Force on Energy Efficiency Standards in Buildings (2018) Mapping of Existing Energy Efficiency Standards and Technologies in Buildings in the UNECE Region; www.unece.org/fileadmin/DAM/hlm/Meetings/2018/09_05-07_St._Petersburg/EE_Standards_in_Buildings_full_version.ENG.pdf

6.9.3 Ethical Consumer, amongst others, has done more detailed work in this area which appears on its website.

6.9.4 Climate change lobby; see e.g. www.theguardian.com/environment/2019/oct/10/vested-interests-public-against-climate-science-fossil-fuel-lobby and https://corporateeurope.org/en/climate-and-energy/2018/11/coal-king-un-climate-talks-poland

Lobbying transparency; https://ec.europa.eu/info/about-european-commission/service-standards-and-principles/transparency/transparency-register_en, and www.opensecrets.org/influence/

www.rapidtransition.org/stories/back-from-the-brink-how-the-world-rapidly-sealed-a-deal-to-save-the-ozone-layer/

Environmental Investigation Agency (2008) Environmental Crime: A threat to our future. https://eia-international.org/wp-content/uploads/reports171-11.pdf

7

PRINCIPLES FOR SMALLER COMPANIES, CHARITIES, AND SOCIAL ENTERPRISES

This chapter looks at principles for smaller organisations, including charities, clubs, social enterprises, companies, and civil society organisations
(CSOs). It is particularly difficult to generalise for a category this wide,
which could range from microbusinesses or local charities with two or
three employees or volunteers, to small and medium-sized enterprises
with perhaps 100 staff. Because of this, for tiny organisations, Chapter 2
on 'Principles for Ordinary Citizens' might be more useful, and for larger
ones or groups manufacturing their own products, Chapter 4 on 'The Role
of Multinational Companies' will have some useful insights too.

7.1 Defining an ethical purchasing policy is a common starting point

Unlike individuals, who can make their ethical buying decisions intuitively
without having to justify them to anybody, organisations sometimes feel
they need a formal written policy to help keep everyone on side. They
aren't always that complicated, but policies with more details are easier
(normally) to apply.

DOI: 10.4324/9781003200185-7

Ethical goals are to some extent normally defined by the nature of the organisation. Children's charities are commonly concerned with supply chain impacts on children, local development groups with the local economy, and environmental groups with environmental impact. Nevertheless, environmental groups and most other organisations rarely want to ignore any harm to children, for example, and children's groups and most other organisations are not usually blasé about climate change either.

There are three key ideas which can help.

7.1.1 Asking questions about what collective campaigns or ethical labels are active makes a good starting point

There's no point in having a policy that cannot be practically implemented. 'All coffee should be Fairtrade' is easier to implement than 'all coffee should avoid child labour', for example. Here is the preamble to Oxfam GB's 2016 ethical purchasing policy:

> In line with our organisational beliefs and values, we only work with suppliers who share our commitment to ethical purchasing. We seek to purchase goods and services that are produced under labour conditions that meet the Ethical Trade Initiative Base Code (ETI) and therefore do not involve the abuse or exploitation of any person. We also seek to work with suppliers who have the least negative impact on climate change and the environment. Prospective suppliers should first read our Ethical and Environmental Policy.

7.1.2 'Stakeholder surveys' to help choose priorities can be useful

We noted in Section 1.8 about how sometimes it is necessary to prioritise one ethical issue over another when tricky issues arise. Because this can involve agreeing on political priorities, wider groups can sometimes usefully input into this. This can range from getting all the staff or members or key customers into a room for half an hour to engaging bigger groups through online questionnaires. This collaborative approach can also serve to strengthen the sense of identity for the communities involved.

7.1.3 'Do no harm' has been a useful basic ethical principle for some groups

Google once used 'don't be evil' as a wider guiding principle. Lots of ethical buying involves 'indirect harm'. If you are buying at a reduced price because of indentured labour or polluting production methods, you could be said to be benefiting from that harm and therefore contributing to it in some way. Major companies, most famously Nike (see Section 3.7.2), used to argue that because the harm was way back in their production chains they were not responsible for it. Ultimately, this position was seen as untenable. Although Google has clearly found 'do no harm' a bit difficult, other companies are still finding it a useful general principle for both their supply chains and elsewhere.

7.1.4 Some companies are moving beyond sustainability into ideas of 'regeneration'

In the 21st century, people are beginning to question whether 'do no harm' is enough and whether there needs to be a new guiding principle more like 'fix broken stuff'. If the world is already so full of problems that we need to be fixing a lot of stuff as we go, do companies need to be looking for suppliers that are actively trying to fix stuff as part of their business models (see also Section 4.6.5)? As part of this discourse, the notion of regenerative business is replacing an older one of sustainable business.

7.2 Looking for opportunities to join collective actions always makes sense

As we have mentioned in Section 1.5, where the organisation is relatively small compared to the supplying companies, working collectively is one of the simplest ways to have a genuinely powerful economic impact.

Collective actions tend to be of three main types:

7.2.1 Boycotts and positive buying campaigns now exist in many consumer product areas

These are the two main product-focussed campaign types which we have discussed in more detail in Chapter 2. We have seen how CSOs have now proliferated in these areas to enable purchasers to act collectively towards common social and environmental goals. These include multi-stakeholder certification schemes like the paper and timber labelling scheme run by the Forest Stewardship Council, campaign groups working to help purchasers identify best practice such as those in the electronics sector like Greenpeace and Electronic Product Environmental Assessment Tool (EPEAT), and collections of purchasers or investors like the Carbon Disclosure Project. We also saw in Section 2.3.4 that it is good to maintain a critical perspective on these projects and that a good guide was looking for the involvement of trusted organisations. It will therefore be useful to ask if there are any such campaigns or schemes already under way in the 'key areas for action' (discussed in Section 7.4).

7.2.2 *Collaborations of ethical purchasers of a particular type are now emerging too*

Trying to decide whether one product is more ethical than another can be technically quite difficult, not least because the product-focussed campaigns don't always agree. As we saw in Chapters 5 and 6, some larger purchaser types have formed collective organisations to help share information. These include US public purchasers, UK university purchasers, and health service green buying initiatives.

But smaller purchasers also collaborate with each other and sometimes have set up green or ethical purchasing networks. For example, some faith groups in the UK, such as the Quakers, have responsible purchasing initiatives and some town councils are collaborating on buying from companies with good tax conduct.

Ethical Consumer Magazine and other publishers of market analyses are also to some extent purchaser collaborations. Ethical Consumer tends to perform critical analyses across a wide range of products. Others, such as the Building Research Establishment's Green Guide to Specification, tend to provide more 'business-to-business' style information in specialist areas. These groups are also covered in Section 2.6.1c.

7.3 Developing a deeper understanding of price is critical to making real impact

As we saw in Section 1.3.3, ethical purchasers take ethical issues into account in addition to price and quality. Indeed, for most, price remains the primary criteria, as it must for all but billionaires. However, we also know that buying on price alone can encourage producers to drive down social and environmental standards (10.1). 'Whole life costing' is one of a number of new concepts which have sprung up to help justify initially higher purchase costs for products with a longer life expectancy (such as low energy light bulbs).

7.3.1 It is useful to look at purchasing as an additional way to make social impact rather than just as a means to an end

For organisations with a social purpose, or even for those with just a distaste for maximising profit at all times, at first sight it may make sense to minimise costs in order to maximise the help that can be given to beneficiaries. However, if purchasing is viewed as a key area in which additional impact may be gained rather than as simply a means to an end, then the idea of always buying the cheapest product is harder to maintain. If an organisation is, for example, also concerned about helping the immediate local area around it, then it may look for opportunities to add local producers to its supplier list.

The notion of Impact Investment has become popular recently. Perhaps, in the future, a similar concept of Impact Purchasing might be developed.

This kind of thinking can become embedded if measuring the amounts of purchase made in ethical ways can be factored into any impact measuring and reporting that is done (see Section 7.7). Of course, asking whether the ends justify the means is one of the oldest philosophical questions we know of, but by and large, those in favour of acting according to ethical principles are not likely to answer this question in the affirmative!

7.3.2 Ethical products are not always the most expensive

For some product areas, there may be 20 or more providers to choose from, such as in coffee and tea. In such areas, there are usually a wide variety of prices, with key ethical products often in the mid-range rather than the most expensive (which are usually designer or luxury brands).

With many potential suppliers, it is usually possible to 'screen out' those failing to meet basic standards and still have a range of options and prices to choose from. This is discussed in more detail in Section 9.4.3.

7.4 Prioritising key areas for action helps to give structure to an ethical purchasing programme

For complex organisations, 'greening a supply chain' or equivalent is often a planned project involving many stages over a number of years (see also Section 4.4.3). Commonly, stage one will identify perhaps ten key supply areas to work on. Key factors normally include:

- amount of spend
- severity of problem or risk
- relative size of the supplier/likelihood of success
- potential for collective action

For micro organisations, it might simply be enough to identify the single most important purchase the organisation makes and to ask the question about whether it could be changed to increase impact. If it takes a year to get this one right, then so be it. Once that decision is comfortably embedded, it will be time to move onto the next one.

7.5 Using the highest quality information available will make the best impact

7.5.1 Certification schemes

Sometimes relatively high quality information is available through certification schemes, such as those discussed Chapter 8. EPEAT and Nordic Swan can, for example, give some information on product environmental impacts in the electronics sector. The need for caution here is a theme running throughout this book (see e.g. 2.3.2–2.3.4).

7.5.2 Supplier surveys

As we can see in Sections 5.7 and 5.8, larger organisations will conduct their own 'supplier surveys', often sending out an annual questionnaire with specific questions pertaining to their own policies. It can be difficult as a small organisation to be taken seriously with this approach, and often the return rates can be very low. A lack of any return though can be an indicator of whether the supplier is really a good one for a long-term relationship. Supplier surveys can also be a useful way of communicating the desire to purchase ethically (see Section 4.9.3(b)).

7.5.3 *Secondary sources*

In many cases, journalistic overviews, such as those available in *Ethical Consumer Magazine* or from Greenpeace in the electronics sector, can provide a starting point for identifying issues and collective projects in a wide range of potential purchase areas.

7.6 Communicating policy goals with suppliers and others is key to effectiveness

A key general principle of ethical purchasing, discussed in Section 1.8, was about how important it is, when thinking of switching suppliers for ethical reasons, to tell them why. We have also just seen in Section 7.5.2 how using supplier surveys can be an indirect way of doing this.

7.6.1 *Working with suppliers to improve standards is also another important option*

As we see later on, when an organisation is bigger than its suppliers or at least a significant customer, education and training can be more effective than simply switching. It is also likely to improve ethics at the supplier's other customers. For tiny businesses and non-governmental organisations, this isn't really a practical option for all but suppliers of an equally small size. For larger organisations though, if the impacts are clearly within their mission, it may be worth exploring this option in more detail (see Section 4.5.2).

Section 1.7 also explains how letting other groups know about any ethical purchasing that is occurring, and encouraging them to do the same, is a useful exercise. This sometimes involves publishing details about ethical purchasing decisions or talking about them at collective gatherings of similar organisations.

7.7 Formally tracking and measuring progress can prevent drift

Unlike larger organisations which can set up bureaucracies to formalise processes, smaller organisations particularly can become distracted from long-term issues by the need to respond to immediate events. Small organisations may simply forget about ethical purchasing programmes or why they are being undertaken.

There are two main solutions to this:

(a) *Regular reporting and review*
     Putting a few lines in each annual report to tell stakeholders what has been done on purchasing in a year can be at least a reminder to review a programme annually.

(b) *Impact measurement*
     Although there is some debate about the value of formally measuring non-financial impacts, with ethical purchasing it is quite easy. This year, for example, we spent £4,000 on Fairtrade coffee supporting farmers in northern Uganda, £12,000 on organic cotton from India for campaign T-shirts, and so on. Combining this kind of impact reporting into annual reports can be an ideal way of reminding everyone why a process is being undertaken.

Tracking and measuring progress is a key principle for most organisations and also discussed in each section on larger purchasing organisations.

References and notes

7.1.1 www.oxfam.org.uk/what-we-do/about-us/plans-reports-and-policies/information-for-suppliers

7.1.2 Stakeholder surveys are a well-trodden path and more information is widely available, including at www.applied-corporate-governance.com/stakeholder-survey/

7.1.3 www.telegraph.co.uk/technology/2018/05/21/google-removes-dont-evil-code-conduct/

7.1.4 Jenny Andersson (2018) What is regenerative business and why do we need it? https://medium.com/activate-the-future/what-is-regenerative-business-3e562f909707

7.2.2 See Trustees' annual report (2016) Britain Yearly Meeting of the Religious Society of Friends (Quakers).
       Tax and local authorities: https://fairtaxmark.net/take-action__trashed/local-council-campaign/.
       Ethical buyers guides: www.ethicalconsumer.org and also www.ethicalconsumer.org/research-hub/global-directory-ethical-consumption

Building research: https://www.bregroup.com/greenguide/podpage.jsp?id=2126

7.3 See e.g. Ing Wong (2010) Whole life costing: Towards a sustainable built environment. *IET Conference Publications.* 10.1049/cp.2010.0442

7.3.2 Ethical Consumer Magazine 179 (November/December 2010) The Price of Ethics

7.5.1 EPEAT Registry. A resource for sustainable electronics: https://epeat.net/

Nordic Swan Ecolabel: The official ecolabel of the Nordic countries. www.nordic-ecolabel.org/

Banktrack is just one group producing a ranking of bank's involvement in fossil fuel funding. www.fossilbanks.org/?bank=anz (Viewed 2/6/19).

8

ETHICAL LABELLING SCHEMES

8.1 Ethical labels or logos have become a key element in helping purchasers to identify more ethical producers

As we saw in Section 2.3.2, ethical labels have become a key way of helping consumers and other purchasers to identify products and services making a wide variety of ethical claims. We saw how labels may be applied to products (e.g. Fairtrade) or to companies (e.g. B-Corporation) and how, in 2017, the Ecolabel Index was tracking 464 labels in 199 countries and across 25 industry sectors.

They may also be variously referred to as sustainability standards and certifications, eco-labels or ethical supply chain certifications.

8.1.1 Ethical labelling schemes grew out of the boycott movements of the late 20th century

Although boycotts (see 2.2.2) were good at telling companies what people didn't like, in complex areas they were less good at explaining what an

DOI: 10.4324/9781003200185-8

acceptable level of ethical performance was. At some stage, campaigners and producers needed to get together to work out what was possible and how it might work in practice where trust had broken down.

Boycotts against unsustainable logging and the emergence of the Forest Stewardship Council (FSC) in the 1990s provide a classic example of the type of compromise that was possible. Disappointed with attempts at international regulation at the UN Earth Summit in Rio in 1992, some environmental groups like Earth First! took to direct action against logging firms, whilst others like Friends of the Earth started boycott campaigns against timber retailers. More mainstream civil society organisations (CSOs) such as World Wide Fund for Nature (WWF) in the UK began to approach businesses to seek a range of commitments. WWF began to draw in other CSOs and the idea was born that a group of CSOs and companies could sit around a table to agree standards. Having the UK's biggest do it yourself retailer at the table, B&Q PLC (formally the target of shop pickets over timber sustainability), was critical for the growth of the FSC label in the UK (see also Section 8.6.1).

8.1.2 They are proliferating because they are a successful model for driving change

One of the basic principles of ethical purchasing, discussed in Chapter 1, is that its effectiveness at driving change is one of the main reasons it is growing. This is particularly the case for ethical labelling schemes which, as we saw in Chapter 2, are generally replacing boycotts as a more focussed approach to trying to create ethical behaviours in companies.

Since 1999, the Ethical Consumer Markets Report has provided an annual measure of (amongst other things) actual sales of ethically labelled products in the UK. The reports have shown a growth in the ethical market from 9 billion in 1999 to 86 billion in 2017. In specific years, sales of products labelled under a particular scheme like Fairtrade or organic may have fallen slightly, but the trend for labelled products overall has risen every year since the measurements began. This is likely to be the case in other countries too.

Because ethical labelling schemes are growing to become quite complex institutions, they now have the resources and motivation to publish detailed accounts of their own impacts. For example, in 2017, Fairtrade International reported in its Annual Monitoring Report that the number of farmers and workers who benefit from programmes had increased by 18%

from the previous year to more than 1.6 million, with premiums paid of around €150 million. They also commissioned more detailed research in the same year called 'The impact of Fairtrade: a review of research evidence 2009–2015' (Darko, Lynch and Smith 2017).

8.1.3 They are also growing because they are an effective way of managing ethical risk for companies

As we discuss in Chapter 9, ethical certifications may not always be used as part of a marketing package for consumers or other purchasers. When this happens, it may be assumed that companies are using certifications as benchmarks or guidelines to help check their approach to ethical issues in their supply chains, and to avoid the risks of public exposure as unethical, which were discussed in Chapter 4. The Better Cotton Initiative (BCI) provides a good example of a place where this approach occurs. BCI is a very successful multi-stakeholder initiative (MSI) with over 1,000 corporate members. It sets environmental and workers' rights standards in cotton production, and Oxfam and WWF were involved in its early development in 2005. In 2017, it claimed that around 14% of global production followed its standards. Although it does have a product label, the majority of its members just use the BCI logo on their websites, in their stores, and in their sustainability reports.

8.2 Ethical labelling schemes normally have four main characteristics: multi-stakeholder governance, standards, audits, and a fee structure

8.2.1 The best ethical labelling schemes will be proper multi-stakeholder initiatives

As we have just observed, the better ethical labelling schemes have generally emerged as an agreement between campaigners and (usually) more enlightened companies on what a more ethical model of production should look like. In order to keep diverse stakeholder groups involved for the long term, they are normally designed with formal roles for each stakeholder type and come in a wide array of arrangements. The FSC has probably the most complex model with a triennial General Assembly of more than 800 groups at the apex. The General Assembly is made up of three chambers: social, environmental, and economic. Voting in each chamber is weighted to ensure that groups from the global North and South each hold 50% of the vote. The Fairtrade Foundation has designated board-level positions for farmer co-ops, while others, like the Rainforest Alliance, may be mainly made up of industry representatives.

As we will see in Section 8.3.3 and elsewhere (see e.g. 2.3.4), it is the degree to which a scheme is genuinely multi-stakeholder which will tend to help consumers and other purchasers determine a transformative scheme from a greenwash-type project.

8.2.2 All ethical labelling schemes require a set of standards to which accredited companies must sign up

Most of us understand that a Fairtrade label on a chocolate bar means that the brand is not being too mean to its suppliers. Some of us may also know that it involves paying a premium to the communities which produce its goods. The reality is that the Fairtrade standards for cocoa producers are pretty complex. They currently run to 23 pages for contract production and cover a wide range of issues, including rules for calculating and transferring the Fairtrade premium. Moreover, this is just one of 77 different UK standards documents covering commodities from bananas to honey and organisations from small producers to employers of hired labour.

And if you think this is complicated, you should see some of the Marine Stewardship Council's (MSC) standards. They have different standards for each of their 280 certified fisheries, and a report on the assessments for just one can run to nearly 300 pages.

Generally, such complex standards are a good thing and reflect the complexity of impacts in bringing products to mass markets in the 21st century. They are almost always publicly available on the websites of ethical labelling schemes.

They are also obviously very technical and as such are the primary area where gathering many stakeholders together in formal groups like 'standards committees' makes sense. We also see in Section 8.3 how it is in this detail where much of the politicking takes place – or indeed where the Devil is to be found!

8.2.3 The impact of a standard on the price of a product will rarely be ignored

Although we look at pricing of ethical products in Chapter 9, it is important to note that most successful schemes are acutely sensitive of the impact of standards on price. In Section 9.4.1, the Fairtrade scheme is used as an example of one which was designed around how much more the majority of purchasers would be willing to pay for its product (around 5–10%). The scheme founders then took this 'surplus' and tried to return it to farmers in the global South.

For others, designing standards which do not cross ethical boundaries is so important that they will price the product at what it costs to produce. This is the case, even if it means that the product costs nearly four times as much as it can sometimes do in the case of organic chicken.

The trade-off between standards which will attract big brands and mass markets or keeping to fundamental ethical principles is at the core of a scheme's identity and always involves some difficult political choices.

8.2.4 Most credible ethical labelling schemes have a system for independently auditing or 'assuring' a company's claims to meet their standards

In Section 4.5.1, we discussed how financial auditing had developed to deal with the problem of trust in a company's own view of its figures, and how social auditing was emerging to deal with a new lack of trust around its ethical claims. In a sense, ethical labelling schemes are an institutionalisation of this development and at their core lie the provision of an independent view on a company's ethical claims. These are normally provided by audit or assurance visits to a production site, which are usually performed regularly (sometimes annually) and which will be formally recorded. Sometimes a certification scheme will have its own auditors, but for the larger schemes they may well outsource them to international firms. As discussed in Chapter 4, this outsourcing has been the source of some criticism.

8.2.5 Almost all ethical labelling schemes will charge a fee to accredited companies to cover the costs of an audit

A fee structure which accredited companies or producers must pay is core to the business models of almost all successful accreditation schemes. Indeed, it is such a successful model that some schemes have grown to become very large institutions. The UK's Soil Association, for example, which is an organic accreditor, had more than £14 million of revenue in 2018 and employed a staff of 253.

The fee model obviously creates a system whereby external assessors have an apparent financial interest in not finding problems that may interfere with future fees. As we discussed under third party auditing (4.5), this problem exists for financial auditing too, but does not prevent its general usefulness. It is also difficult to see how else (with the exception of government funding) a scheme might be economically viable.

8.3 Ethical labelling schemes are essentially political projects

At this point in the story, it would be tempting to suggest that ethical labels are an unremittingly positive contribution to the world of ethical consumption. The trouble with this is that, as we have seen at other stages in this book, not all ethical labels are great. One way of understanding why is to see them as they are: essentially political projects. And the nature of their political purpose can be divided into two main types:

(a)   *They are political, in the broader sense that they are all saying the free market is not delivering desirable outcomes for everyone.*

They are all saying that business as usual isn't working in some particular way – or why would they need to exist? So they are essentially proposals for new or modified models of production. We call them ethical labelling schemes rather than political labelling schemes because they are often dealing (or claiming to deal) with widely agreed fundamental standards (see Section 1.1.3). For example, on fairness, they will commonly say that workers should generally have International Labour Organisation standards in the workplace, and on sustainability, they tend to say that business should have models which build in the cost of sustaining the ecosystems in which they operate.

(b) *They are also political in the smaller sense, in that choosing the point at which we can say that these particular standards are good enough for fairness or sustainability can be a tricky call.*

This is best illustrated by the proliferation of labels certifying the same thing in slightly different ways. In timber, for example, an Indonesian company could certify against one of four acronyms: FSC, PEFC, LEI, and SVLK. And in palm oil, there is also a range of standards, including the Roundtable on Sustainable Palm Oil (RSPO), the Sustainable Agriculture Network (SAN) and the Roundtable on Sustainable Biomaterials (RSB). Workers' rights also appear as key elements in many standards, including Fairtrade, Rainforest Alliance, UTZ, and the Global Organic Textile Standard (GOTS).

Another theme in this book is that, predictably perhaps, we find that purchasers would prefer fewer and better ethical labels (see 2.6.1). Like political parties though, people have found it easier to set up many small factions than to agree general principles in a few broad groupings. Monty Python's film *Life of Brian*, which satirised this human weakness through the People's Front of Judea and the Judean People's Front, has become a classic expression of this tendency. In some cases, setting up competing schemes is a deliberate political tactic created by companies to try to control, and often reduce, the ethical standards expected of them, which we look at in the sections immediately below.

8.3.1 Some company or government-led ethical labelling schemes look designed to slow the rate of change

The classic case occurred in 1999 with the arrival of the Programme for the Endorsement of Forest Certification (PEFC) to offer a more business-friendly alternative to the successful FSC scheme which began in 1993. A Greenpeace report from 2011 stated: "The PEFC system was established by the forest and wood products industry, and the governance structure reflects this with the balance of power sitting with industry representation." In the same report, it is argued that the limited role given to non-government organisations (NGOs) in the International Stakeholder Members group discouraged many environmentally focused NGOs from engaging with PEFC. The report also raised serious questions about PEFC's auditing procedure.

The timing of the establishment of the PEFC, set up after the arrival of the successful NGO-led scheme FSC, does look like a blatant attempt to create a competitor with lower standards to reduce the commercial impacts of the other scheme.

It should also be noted that sometimes governments can become involved in setting up rival schemes with lower standards too. This has occurred with palm oil certifications brought forward by the Indonesian and Malaysian governments.

8.3.2 Other company-led schemes make no attempt to bring in other stakeholders

In the UK, big industrial farming has a very powerful lobby group called the National Farmers Union (NFU). In 2000, it introduced the Red Tractor assurance label as a guarantee of quality and welfare standards in meat production. The animal welfare standards it assures are rarely greater than those required by UK law. Unsurprisingly, no welfare organisations were engaged in the organisation of this scheme, and though it has the other three characteristics of an ethical label, it makes no attempt to be a multi-stakeholder project.

The NFU argues that it serves a useful purpose for some consumers, because the cages that the UK government permits for say laying hens are slightly larger than those permitted by some other countries which UK consumers can buy from. Campaigners are also able to note the emergence of the Red Tractor label after the rapid growth of the organic label (begun in 1973) and the Royal Society for the Prevention of Cruelty to Animals (RSPCA)-assured label (begun in 1994).

8.3.3 It is sometimes useful to distinguish between campaigner-led and producer-led initiatives or to describe all ethical labelling schemes as being on a spectrum between company dominated at one end and campaigner dominated at the other

Since ethical labelling schemes are essentially political projects, asking whether ethical labelling schemes are good is a bit like asking whether political parties are good. Some, the ones you agree with, will be good. For a while at least! Others will be terrible.

In reality, it is less common to find successful schemes that are totally dominated by one or other camp, because to do so in the longer term will affect commercial viability. They are useful for companies only because they can help deflect external ethical criticisms by showing that some action is being taken, and for campaigners they are only useful in driving change if a lot of companies sign up.

In this way, all schemes will appear on a spectrum, from totally company dominated at one end (like Red Tractor) to totally campaigner dominated at the other (like for example Ethical Consumer Research Association's own Best Buy label). The spectrum can also help illustrate the political tension within most schemes. Big companies may be trying to pull it in one direction to make it easier to certify their products, whilst campaigners may be resisting in order to protect the interests of other stakeholders.

Although quite a lot of proliferation of labels around the same commodity occurs when companies set up competing schemes with lower standards, it should be noted that it is not always one-way traffic. The Palm Oil Innovation Group was set up in 2013 with higher standards than the RSPO, in an open attempt to lobby their larger rival to tighten up their standards.

8.3.4 Sometimes there are attempts at coalition building

Not all political movements fracture into different bickering factions, and sometimes it is possible to observe counter trends like consolidation and coalition building. In 2018, the merger between Rainforest Alliance and UTZ brought a significant consolidation in the certification landscape. It was welcomed by some producers who were pleased that costs would fall because they would not need to be certified twice. Campaigners however were worried that the merger of standards would result in the lowest being adopted in each situation where there was an overlap.

In 2007, when the BCI was formed, the founders took some care to align their new standards with some pre-existing ones in Australia and Brazil. And in the 1990s, there were even discussions between the Fairtrade and Organic movements in the UK to see if a standard could be agreed for UK farmers treating workers fairly. In the end, it was not successful but it was the right question to ask.

8.4 Ethical labelling schemes are frequently the target of criticism and debate

Taking a position in the real world on the point at which, for example, support for workers or sustainable forests becomes significant enough to deserve a label will always be controversial. As we have discussed above, for campaigners it will rarely be moving forward quickly enough, and companies may want to argue that it is too expensive to adopt without having to implement significant price increases. So companies and campaigners, both within and outside whatever multi-stakeholder 'tent' a scheme has managed to create, will both be pushing all the time to get their views heard. This is entirely appropriate and it is what politics is all about.

Indeed, it could be said that the locus of political debate on ethical issues in international supply chains has now moved significantly towards ethical labelling schemes and away from parliaments, which for various reasons (see 1.4.2) have trouble regulating in this space anyway. These debates can be quite technical, but like all political discourse it is ideal that it takes place transparently or in public view as much as is possible. This, unfortunately, is not always the case.

In addition, the whole idea of ethical labelling schemes themselves has come under attack, and we look at criticisms from the right and left separately below.

8.4.1 Some criticisms can be characterised as coming from the ideological right

As we saw in 8.3(a), all ethical labelling schemes are political, in the broader sense that they are all saying the free market is not delivering desirable outcomes for everyone. This means that for many people on the ideological right, they are all problematic.

In the UK, the classic example of this kind of attack occurred in 2008 when the Adam Smith Institute sent out researchers into Fairtrade certified supply chains to try to find transgressions from the standards that would discredit the whole scheme. However, their deeper agenda was clearly to attack the idea that markets were failing in some respects.

In their report "Fair Trade is Unfair," they expanded on a number of criticisms and said:

> Fair trade does not aid economic development. It keeps the poor in their place, sustaining uncompetitive farmers on their land and holding back diversification, mechanization, and moves up the value chain. This denies future generations the chance of a better life.

Although this resulted in some sympathetic articles in newspapers, including the Daily Telegraph, generally the coverage noted where the report had come from and saw it for what it was. Despite this and other attacks, the Fairtrade scheme continues to flourish today.

Defending themselves and their certified companies from political criticism is therefore one of the core purposes of an ethical labelling scheme.

8.4.2 Other criticisms come more from the ideological left

There is long history of academic criticism of certification schemes, but as with criticisms from the right, it is just as instructive to look at one.

The campaigning research group Changing Markets Foundation published a report in 2018 called "The false promise of certification." In it, they were mainly looking in detail at problem schemes certifying palm oil and sustainable fishing. However, they also had some general criticisms. We can categorise these into two main types.

(a)   *One is that schemes are never preferable to regulation.*

They said: "While voluntary initiatives and certification can play a role in driving more sustainable practices, this report also concludes that they cannot – and should not – replace governmental and international regulations." In a sense, this is not the fault of the schemes themselves, but a practical problem with regulating global supply chains, which we have discussed extensively elsewhere.

(b)   *The second type of criticism is that many powerful schemes appear to be too much at the company dominated end of the spectrum we discussed above.*

They said: The main conclusion of this report is that certification has lost its way and that its contribution to creating a more sustainable world is minute. We argue that it can even cause active damage; it lowers the bar to certify higher product volumes and in many cases fails to enforce greater transparency, thereby providing cover for unsustainable companies and practices.

As we see below, this type of problem appears to be creating alliances of civil society groups to act as a single voice against this problem.

8.4.3 The third type of criticism are best characterised as technical

These criticisms focus on specific weakness in the standards themselves or in their practical implementation.

There are, for example, sometimes concerns expressed around the 'materiality' of standards. This asks whether a label is just looking at one particular aspect of a supply chain or whether it is more holistically seeking to ensure most problem areas in a product are addressed. For example, the sustainable forest label 'Canopy Style' has been criticised for giving a positive label to clothing companies whose garment factories further down the supply chain were highly polluting. The Fairtrade cotton label has also come in for criticism when, in certifying cotton producers, it applied labels to finished clothes which had not asked questions about whether sweat-shop labour was used in its stitching factories.

Around standards and assessment methods, there has also been criticism of schemes which certify on a 'mass balance' basis. This means that so long as a company can show that, for example, 30% of the cocoa it bought was certified, it can certify 30% of its products without having to guarantee that a particular product contains a particular certified ingredient.

We have also discussed elsewhere criticisms of audit impartiality and high prices for certification being barriers to access (8.4).

8.4.4 We are beginning to see the emergence of formal coalitions of civil society groups designed to lobby some of the biggest schemes

Some of the more successful labelling schemes have now become quite large bureaucracies. The Rainforest Alliance, for example, had revenues of $41 million in 2017, the Soil Association had revenues of £16 million, and the Marine Stewardship Council had revenues of £20 million in the same year. Some civil society groups, like Greenpeace, are large enough to be a powerful critic of problem schemes on their own. For smaller civil society groups, which believe that some schemes are not moving far enough and fast enough, there appears to be an emerging pattern of forming coalitions in order to create enough pressure to have influence.

The first formal organisation designed to lobby a single scheme was FSC Watch set up in 2006, and its detailed critiques have become a model for others to follow. Since then, there is an emerging tendency for more formal coalitions to emerge. For example, there were 58 marine conser-vation groups listed in 2019 as partners on the campaigning website at www.make-stewardship-count.org, which is calling for "urgent and swift changes to the MSC certification standard in order to uphold the scientific rigour, transparency, and original vision of the seafood label."

Elsewhere, there is co-ordinated lobbying around human rights certi-fications too. In the USA, the Fair World Project exists to lobby and track the practices of the growing number of fair trade schemes there, and in the UK, Ethical Consumer organised an open letter campaign with 13 other Civil Society Organisations around the merger of the UTZ and Rainforest Alliance schemes in 2018.

From a resource point of view, monitoring scheme behaviours and campaigning for change is a difficult task for small campaign groups to take on. This is another area where collective or government resources could be useful.

8.5 Proliferation has led to civil society initiatives to help purchasers identify the best ethical labels

We saw in Section 2.6.1 how ethical labels had become an important short cut or ways to deal with complexity for many consumers. We also saw in 2.3.2 how consumer surveys showed that consumers were becoming baffled by the proliferation of competing labels and that they would prefer fewer and better ones. Principle 2.3.4 went on to say that spotting the best ethical labels will usually involve looking for the involvement of a campaign group that individuals trust and that transparency was also a good quality indicator in this space.

There are three formal approaches that civil society groups have developed to navigate this territory.

8.5.1 There is now a certification scheme for certification schemes

In 2002, partly to try to address the emergence of problem schemes, a group of ethical labelling schemes got together to try to establish standards for this sector. The International Social and Environmental Accreditation and Labeling (ISEAL) Alliance's stated mission is "to strengthen sustainability standards systems for the benefit of people and the environment."

It has ten "Credibility Principles" which are: sustainability; (continuous) improvement; relevance; rigour; engagement; impartiality; transparency; accessibility; truthfulness; and efficiency. It also provides a range of detailed guidance documents to help apply these principals in the real world.

It only had 19 members in 2019 from the potentially 466 listed on ecolabel.com. However, its members include some of the biggest and most significant projects. They include some well-regarded schemes like Fairtrade International as well as some like the RSPO and MSC, which have become so widely criticised around specific accreditations that they have spawned their own opposition coalitions (8.4.3).

Whilst it is very reasonable to try to gather rational criteria together to try to identify quality, the presence of very controversial projects on the member lists continue to show how difficult it is to solve complex political problems just by getting the process criteria right.

8.5.2 Some consumers associations are beginning to rank ethical labels too

Formal projects to rank labels have now been set up in a few countries, including Germany, Austria, and the USA. The German website label-online.de was launched in 2000, and has since been funded by the German Federal Ministry for the Environment, the Federal Environment Agency, and the Federal Ministry of Food and Agriculture. The website and mobile app is linked to a database of national, regional, and international labels. On the surface, at least, the four main principles it applies to its scoring (standard, independence, control, and transparency) look slightly different to those of ISEAL: the control and independence elements perhaps looking more closely at business dominance.

ECRA in the UK has also been working in this area for decades, and since 2013 uses six main criteria: governance and funding; membership and beneficiaries; assessment methods; areas of criticism; visibility; and transparency. Like the advice in 2.3.4, ECRA is mainly looking for campaign groups it trusts within MSIs. For consumers, ECRA argues that most MSIs provide some degree of trust that a supply chain is managed with ethics in mind and can provide a practical market choice for some people. As we have seen though, not all labels purporting to be ethical are however genuinely multi-stakeholder.

Ecolabel.org (mentioned in 8.1) also records some quality characteristics such as standard-setting and compliance. However, these details are behind a paywall and do not appear to comment on quality variations.

8.5.3 Campaign groups are publishing their own guides to ethical labels too

Some single-issue civil society groups are also trying to help raise standards in certification by providing consumer advice in the specific areas in which they work. The UK animal welfare group Compassion in World Farming, for example, publishes a 'Compassionate food guide' which ranks food labels on a 100-point scale. They use their own list of preferred standards such as 'freedom to express normal behaviour' to ascribe a value to the extent to which each scheme can guarantee that such standards are met.

The Fair World Project, mentioned in 8.4.4, also publishes an *International Guide to Fair Trade Labels*. Published in 2015 (and updated in 2020) and 125 pages long, it provides a detailed analysis and ultimately an opinion on the performance of nine labels across a variety of criteria.

It should be noted that governments have also become involved in providing advice in this area (see also Section 6.4). Disappointingly, but perhaps not surprisingly, in their attempts to avoid political controversy their advice can be less useful as a driver for change. The UK government's Timber Procurement Policy's treatment of FSC and PEFC as equivalent is a case in point.

8.6 Characterising ethical labelling schemes as voluntary initiatives is useful to some degree but does not always tell the whole story

Some political commentators characterise ethical labelling schemes as voluntary initiatives. Typically, when a government wants to regulate a particular corporate behaviour, it will speak to the companies first. Well-organised industries will commonly offer to adopt a voluntary 'code of practice' in order to head off 'unnecessary' regulation. Tobacco advertising codes of practice, which emerged in the 1960s in the UK and USA, are one classic example of where this approach took place. Generally speaking, corporate codes are seen by campaigners as a poor second best option to regulation since they may be frequently flouted with relative impunity. This was indeed the case with the tobacco advertising codes, and regulation was eventually adopted to prevent further transgressions.

8.6.1 Purely voluntary codes are less likely to have civil society organisations involved in their design

Although all ethical labelling schemes are essentially voluntary, it is obviously a different thing for companies to sign up to code of their own design, to choosing to join a scheme set up by campaigners to try to stop picket lines or banner drops outside their stores damaging their brand's reputation. As we saw in Section 8.1.2, B&Q PLC, a key player in the emergence of the FSC label in the UK, came to the table after years of being targeted by campaigners over unsustainable timber in its supply chain. The Rainforest Action Group in the UK in 1991 had a giant inflatable chainsaw which it set up in B&Q car parks with a 'chainsaw massacre' banner beside it. At the same time, members of Earth First! would perform citizens' arrests on 'illegal' timber in store, which involved carrying it out without paying and waiting to be arrested themselves.

8.6.2 Purely voluntary codes are less likely to have third party auditing, reporting, and transparency

As we saw in 8.2.4, one of the main characteristics of the better ethical label-ling schemes is that they will have some kind of regular (usually annual) auditing and reporting procedure to check whether a company is indeed adhering to the promised set of new standards. This approach is much less likely to be present in purely company-driven codes. Indeed, it was not present in the Tobacco Advertising codes of the 1970s we mentioned above. After all, why would companies voluntarily set up a bureaucracy who will collect and publish data showing how they are failing to meet standards in some respects, unless they were to some degree being forced to?

What we are saying here is that if we go back to the idea that ethical labelling schemes are on a spectrum from company led to campaigner led, those at the company led end can be properly described as voluntary initia-tives and for those at the campaigner led end can be that something a bit more complicated is going on.

8.6.3 Some commentators have used the term 'civil regulation' to describe the role that 'voluntary' labelling schemes are beginning to take

The rise of certification means that at any given time, whole teams of 'inspectors' will be visiting production sites around the world and report-ing on what they have found. In many cases, this may result in presenting manufacturers or growers with a set of 'remedial actions' or measures they need to take to maintain the label in the following year.

Some academics have noted that this doesn't look too different to the activities of factory inspectors employed by governments to perform a similar task, and have therefore employed the term 'civil regulation' to describe what they are seeing. The use of the term regulation contrasts sharply with the notion of voluntarism.

Like ethical labelling schemes, government inspectors might issue a small fine for transgression, but will also commonly agree to a course of remedial actions with an employer as an alternative to immediate sanction. Also, like the more problematic ethical labelling schemes, there is unfortunately a long history of government inspectors turning a blind eye to transgressions if the economic incentives are right.

8.6.4 Some ethical labelling schemes are government led and not voluntary

In Section 6.6.1(a), we saw how governments can require companies to label their products with elements which contain information for prospective ethical purchasers. The European A-G energy labelling scheme is one such example. Another is the requirement for food companies in the EU to label any product containing genetically modified ingredients.

Confusingly, governments can also be involved in supporting or creating purely voluntary labels which companies can apply for. The European eco-label (flower) is one example of this type of voluntary government scheme.

In addition, and as we will see in the section that follows, there are a number of ways in which governments do work with ethical labelling schemes to make them more effective.

8.7 Better government intervention around ethical labelling and certification schemes could help the sector

8.7.1 Some interventions are already happening

Section 6.8 looked at interventions which governments could make to help support ethical purchasing more generally. Those which impacted ethical labelling schemes included:

(a)   Using government buying to reward excellence

Sometimes this is disappointing for campaigners (around sustainable timber in the UK for example), who feel that governments are setting the bar too low.

(b)   Publishing government research into the best ethical approaches

We saw this, for example, with the German state-funded label ranking project in 8.5.2.

(c)   *Regulating ethical claims*

This does happen occasionally. The UK's Advertising Standards Authority, for example, did uphold a 2012 complaint against a Red Tractor Scheme advert claiming that the pork products it certified were 'high welfare pork'.

(d)   *Providing financial support for the better schemes*

The UK Department for International Development (DFID) has provided some financial support for Fairtrade and associated projects in the UK over the years. Similar support for Fairtrade has occurred throughout Europe. Organic labelling schemes have also received support. UK and European governments have provided financial support for farms 'in transition' − a period where farmers stop using certain chemicals but before they get full organic certification. This has helped the proportion of organically farmed land to grow to 7.3% in Germany, 7.0% in France, and 2.6% in the UK.

8.7.2 *Further interventions could be useful*

The Changing Markets report in Section 8.4.2 suggested that some schemes were so bad that they should be banned. While it may be interesting to speculate how this could be technically possible with globally produced and distributed products, it is generally easier to use 'softer' incentives such as a battery of those that are already being used (a-d) above. It also feels a bit like banning political activity, which in general is rightly frowned upon by liberal opinion. However, there are precedents to interventions restricting large companies from both ordinary political activity and anti-competitive practices, which might be useful here.

The Changing Markets report concludes by calling for reforms to be based on the following four principles:

1. **Transparency** includes availability of criteria and reporting on the performance of different members of the scheme, and encourages supply chain transparency.
2. **Independence** includes removing conflicts of interest, such as decoupling membership revenue from certification and compliance outcomes, and ensuring independent bodies set the standards.
3. **Holistic approach with high traceability**, aiming to cover the whole life cycle of a product, and not allowing companies to pick and choose criteria or to be certified with conditions.

4. **Aiming for continuous improvements** includes setting the bar high enough to only certify companies that demonstrably go above and beyond average performance and are committed to continuous improvement.

Comfortingly, these principles are not altogether dissimilar from those discussed in Section 8.5 looking at trying to find quality in this crowded field.

References and notes

8.1.2 R. Harrison (2005) Pressure Groups, Campaigners and Consumers in Rob Harrison, Terry Newholm and Deirdre Shaw (eds.) *The Ethical Consumer.* Sage. London.

D.F. Murphy and J. Bendell (2001). Getting engaged: Business-NGO relations sustainable development, in *The Earthscan Reader in Business and Sustainable Development*, Edited by R. Starkey and R. Welford. Earthscan. London.

8.1.3 Ethical Consumer Markets Reports; see https://www.ethicalconsumer. org/research-hub/uk-ethical-consumer-markets-report

E. Darko, A. Lynch, and W. Smith (2017) The impact of Fairtrade: A review of research evidence 2009–2015; www.odi.org/publications/10891-impact-fairtrade-review-research-evidence-2009-2015

8.1.4 https://bettercotton.org/bci-2017-annual-report-reveals-better-cotton-now-accounts-for-14-of-global-cotton-production/

8.2.1 https://ic.fsc.org/en/what-is-fsc/governance/general-assembly

Marine Stewardship Council. See e.g. Final Report on the Re assessment of the Russian Federation Barents Sea cod, haddock and saithe fishery (MSC 2019)

8.2.3 www.reuters.com/article/us-money-chicken-organic/is-organic-chicken-worth-the-price-idUSKBN0FM24Q20140717

8.2.4 Lars H. Gulbrandsen (2008) Accountability arrangements in non-state standards organizations: Instrumental design and imitation. *Organisation*, 15(4), pp. 563–583. Sage Journals.

8.2.5 www.soilassociation.org/media/19401/annual-report-accounts-2019.pdf

Audit problems are endemic, but see e.g. www.washingtonpost.com/business/2019/10/23/chocolate-companies-say-their-cocoa-is-certified-some-farms-use-child-labor-thousands-are-protected-forests/

Clean Clothes Campaign (2005) Looking for a quick fix – How weak social auditing is keeping workers in sweatshops; https://cleanclothes.org/file-repository/resources-publications-05-quick-fix.pdf

8.3 Palm oil certification is discussed in detail in The False Promise of Certification – Changing Markets Foundation May 2018

ILO standards in social labels; www.epsu.org/article/social-and-ethical-labels

8.3.1 Greenpeace and others (2011) On The Ground 2011 The controversies of PEFC and SFI https://mobil.wwf.de/fileadmin/user_upload/PDF/On_The_Ground_2011.pdf.

Critiques of the Indonesian and Malaysian governments' palm oil certification appear in the False Promise of Certification above.

8.3.2 www.ciwf.org.uk/philip-lymbery/blog/2015/06/why-george-monbiot-is-right-about-red-tractor

8.3.3 Read about the Palm Oil Innovation Group at www.poig.org

8.3.4 www.ethicalconsumer.org/food-drink/open-letter-rainforest-alliance-utz

https://bettercotton.org/about-bci/bci-history/

Fairtade and Organic UK standard – conversations with the author 1997.

8.4.1 Marc Sidwell (2008) Unfair trade. Available as a pdf from www.adamsmith.org/blog/international/unfair-trade. The *Guardian*'s comment on it at https://www.theguardian.com/theguardian/2008/mar/08/2

The *Telegraph* 25/2/08; www.telegraph.co.uk/news/uknews/1579776/Fairtrade-harms-third-world-farmers.html

8.4.2 Sally Eden (2011) The politics of certification: consumer knowledge, power, and global governance in ecolabelling, in *Global Political Ecology*, Edited by Richard Peet, Paul Robbins, and Michael Watts. Routledge. London.

The False Promise of Certification. Changing Markets Foundation May 2018.

8.4.3 Canopy Style is criticised in False Promise cited above;

https://cleanclothes.org/news/2016/03/22/new-fairtrade-standard-will-not-benefit-garment-workers

www.triplepundit.com/story/2015/mass-balance-pushing-your-chocolate-bar-too-far/35231

8.4.4 https://fsc-watch.com

https://fairworldproject.org

www.ethicalconsumer.org/food-drink/open-letter-rainforest-alliance-utz

8.5.1 www.isealalliance.org/community-members?f%5B0%5D=community_status%3A176

8.5.2 https://label-online.de/
www.ethicalconsumer.org/research-hub/ethical-accreditation-schemes

8.5.3 https://assets.ciwf.org/media/7432869/compassionate_food_guide_web_download.pdf

https://fairworldproject.org/wp-content/uploads/2019/12/international-Guide-to-Fair-Trade-Labels-2020-Edition.pdf

8.6 For an example of the use of voluntary in the discourse, see Muradian and Pelupessy (2005) Governing the coffee chain: The role of voluntary regulatory systems. *World Development*, 33(12), pp. 2029–2044.

The role on voluntary codes in tobacco; see e.g. www.sourcewatch.org/index.php/Voluntary_codes

8.6.1 *Ethical Consumer Magazine*. Issue number 15. August 1991.

8.6.3 David Vogel (February 2010) Taming globalization? Civil regulation and corporate capitalism, in *The Oxford Handbook of Business and Government*, Edited by David Coen, Wyn Grant, and Graham Wilson. Oxford: Oxford University Press.

J. Bendell (2001e) Civil regulation – how nonprofits are co-regulating business in a global economy. *Non-Profit Quarterly*, 8(4).

8.7.1 *Guardian* 2012; www.theguardian.com/media/2012/aug/29/pork-not-porkies-ads-banned

Government funding for Fairtrade: *Guardian* August 2012: "Fairtrade 'disappointed' by government's commitment to ethical trade movement". www.theguardian.com/business/2007/dec/24/ethicalbusiness.ethicalliving

For UK government support for conversion to organic farming, see e.g. https://data.gov.uk/dataset/f79c982a-761f-4c2f-88a7-cc732655add3/organic-farming-scheme-agreements

EU organic farming statistics 2018; https://ec.europa.eu/eurostat/statistics-explained/index.php/Organic_farming_statistics

8.7.2 US restrictions on political funding are listed here: www.fec.gov/help-candidates-and-committees/candidate-taking-receipts/contribution-limits/

9

SELLING TO ETHICAL PURCHASERS

9.1 To transition to ethical economies it is also important to pay attention to the supply side

(a) *Consumer markets*

In principle (9.2), we look at the evidence which suggests that the majority of people express an interest in buying ethically. If this is the case, transforming to economies where the majority of goods are ethically produced is not a matter of persuading more people to buy ethically, because they already want to do this. It is a matter of making it possible for people to choose widely available and good quality ethical products. In other words, it means that the 'supply side', as economists call it, needs addressing too.

The link between availability and mass participation is regularly identified in the annual survey of UK ethical markets carried out by Ethical Consumer Research Association. For example, very significant growth in the sale of Fairtrade-certified products occurred in the period after 2008 when the cane sugar multinational Tate & Lyle, whose products are distributed to every corner shop in the country, announced its intention to certify the whole of its retail sugar cane

DOI: 10.4324/9781003200185-9

production supply chain. Similar big growths in sales of ethically certified products have occurred when other large companies decided to change their approach. Unilever's adoption of the Rainforest Alliance certification for its best-selling PG Tips tea brand in 2007 had a similar effect in the UK tea market. Whether these are properly 'ethical purchases' when people may not even be aware that they have made an ethical choice is a question for theologians, but for campaigners who are looking to drive change the question is of less concern.

(b) *Institutional purchasers*

We have also seen how large institutional purchasers including companies (Chapter 4) and governments (Chapters 5 and 6) can have complex ethical purchasing programmes. They can also proactively work with their supply chains to introduce ethical standards to meet their own specific ethical demands.

The discussions in this chapter mainly focus on consumers, since this is where much of the market research around ethical choices can be found. Nevertheless, the learnings around the importance of price and quality particularly are just as important for companies supplying institutional buyers.

(c) *Product as campaign*

We also see (9.6) how supplying an 'ethical' product can in some cases be a campaigning act, particularly if the purchasers are not aware that the ethical issue in question needs to be addressed.

9.2 The majority of consumers express interest in ethical issues

When people first began discussing the idea of ethical or green consumers in the late 1980s, some companies began by assuming that it was a 'niche market' of slightly strange people that could be 'targeted' in the same way as other niches, like Goths or gay Australians. Because there was money to be made, opinion surveys began to be commissioned which sought to try to identify how to find this niche. The results didn't go as expected (Figure 9.1).

Always ethical	Sometimes ethical	Can't be bothered
5-10%	60-75%	20-30%

Figure 9.1 Consolidated survey data on consumer ethical buying intentions 1989–2018.

With 60%–75% of people expressing an interest in ethical buying, it was clearly not a niche in the normal sense. The chart above, also reproduced at Section 1.3, summarises the broad results of opinion surveys asking whether people wanted to buy ethical products across a range of issues tracked since 1989 by Ethical Consumer. It also noted how these results were reproduced across different cultures and countries all around the world.

Although we talk about how reliable these surveys are at Section 9.9, being wary about any discussion of ethical purchasers which does treat them as a niche is the first step in understanding this set of behaviours.

This majority of people, classed as 'sometimes ethical', will buy an ethical product or join a boycott if they see it, but are not consciously looking out for ethical choices across everything they do.

9.2.1 It is possible to break this 70% down into different subtypes

(a)   The 'super ethical' 5%–10%

Essentially, this group, also recognised on the chart above, is making a conscious attempt to make ethical choices consistently across most of what they buy and do. Academics have spent quite a lot of time understanding this group. Environmental concerns and green politics, which take the idea of individual responsibility seriously, are often at the heart of this more consistent approach. It would be a mistake though to think that this consistency means that they are not as price-sensitive as other buying types (see Section 9.3). This group is not normally any more affluent than those in other categories.

(b)   Subtypes of concern can be identified around specific ethical issues

At Ethical Consumer, researchers have grouped the main issues of concern to UK consumers into:

Environmental
Human rights
Animal welfare
Political activity
Product sustainability

Each of these can be further broken down into different types. Environment, for example, contains subsections on Palm Oil, Habitats,

Climate Change, and Pollution. Many consumer surveys have asked questions at this level of subtypes. Broadly speaking, environmental and human rights concerns tend to poll at around 60%–70% levels of concern, with other issues still significant and rarely falling below 40%. Ethical Consumer's top level criteria are listed in a little more detail in Appendix A3.

(c)   *There is some evidence of a division between global and local concerns*

Of the 70% of 'sometimes ethical', there is some evidence that, in the UK at least, they can be divided into two main subtypes. Around half are concerned with the type of global issues of social justice and environmental impact that multinational supply chains often bring up. Another half are more concerned with issues closer to home. These will also be around the same broad issues, but more focussed on local impacts, such as poor treatment of workers, animals, or local environments.

(d)   *Other demographics*

Unsurprisingly, companies also want to know about whether ethical choices are more likely to be found in women or men, or older or younger people. By and large, there is little consistent evidence of any significant variations regarding these core demographics. There are some exceptions to this in specific areas though. A big rise in veganism among 'millennials' (25–35 years old) globally attracted a lot of attention in 2018, for example.

(e)   *Changes over time*

The other, perhaps obvious, point to note is that these characteristics are not fixed.

First, issues of concern can come and go. Whilst there was a consumer boycott campaign against some South African producers in the 1970s, this came to an end with the ending of the apartheid system in 1992. Similarly, Palm Oil production was not an identifiable issue of international concern in 1992, but was at the forefront of many people's minds in 2017.

Second, people can move from one type to another during their lifetimes. Some people in 'can't be bothered' can undergo a damascene conversion and move to the 'always ethicals', whilst others – perhaps because of an external event like a family health crisis – can move in the other direction.

9.2.2 It is possible that rising ethical purchasing creates more ethical purchasing

If discussions of ethical purchasing choices are more frequent or become normalised, then these may of themselves encourage more people to think in this way, or more people to consider moving from the sometimes ethicals to the always ethicals. The possibility of virtuous circles operating in this space is discussed further in Sections 10.7.4 and 10.8.2.

9.3 It is important for sellers to focus on price and quality first

In Section 1.3, under basic principles, we noted how one of the key characteristics of ethical purchasers is that they are looking at ethics in addition to price and quality. We explained that:

> one of the most common misunderstandings about ethical purchasing is that ethics is the primary concern when this kind of purchasing takes place. Although this is the case in some circumstances, in the majority of cases ethics is a third factor once information on price (what is affordable) and quality (what works) has been weighed up.

In the early 1990s, when the idea of green or ethical buying first emerged, a lot of new products were launched which, although they addressed ethical issues, were frankly not very good. Most noticeably, perhaps, were the ethical coffees which tasted like sawdust and the ethical cleaning products which didn't clean very well. Unsurprisingly, they were not very commercially successful.

Pricing is discussed in some detail in Section 9.4 because there is some complexity to explore. With quality, the lessons are simple and unexceptional. Successful products, ethical or otherwise, need great quality.

9.3.1 Some producers aiming for mass markets have tried removing ethical stories from the marketing mix

Towards the end of the 1990s in the UK, some successful ethical brands began looking at how they could grow their market share beyond what they saw as the 'always ethicals' niche. They did some consumer research which suggested that some people were viewing ethical claims as an indicator of lower quality and potentially of higher price too. It is possible that this was a learned experience from the period of dodgy ethical coffee and problem detergents. Either way, they changed their marketing approach and focussed on extolling the great price or quality of what they offered. Cafédirect (Fairtrade) coffee focussed on its taste, the Phone Co-op focussed on its customer service, and the Co-op Bank focussed on its prices and service. Ethical claims were not removed altogether in every case, but moved down in the 'marketing mix' to perhaps the third or fourth item. Whilst this approach did work for a while, there are some disadvantages to it. First, as we see in Section 9.7, it can work less well in markets where the majority of products have some ethical claims attached. It also removes the possibility to achieve campaigning or awareness-raising goals with ethical product marketing (see Section 9.6).

Perhaps one of the most useful effects of this story is as a lesson or reminder of the obvious fact that if you can't focus on price and quality first, the likely success of ethical products will be strictly limited.

9.4 The pricing of 'ethical' products is critical to their success

9.4.1 Generally speaking, the majority of buyers will only pay perhaps 5% or 10% more for an ethical product

As we saw in Section 8.2.3, when the Fairtrade Foundation was set up in the UK at the beginning of the 1990s, it did extensive research into how much more people were willing to pay for a fairly traded product. The maximum increase that the 'sometimes ethicals' (see Section 9.2) or the bulk of the consumer market would tolerate at that time was around 10%. They therefore designed a standard that would, on average, lead to products which cost only around 10% more than mainstream brands. The idea was that if this additional cost was returned to farmers in the global South, it could make a significant impact. They felt that the scheme, if successful, could also work at scale with whole consumer markets changing to this model. To some degree, they have seen this approach work.

This survey response to willingness to pay more for ethical products tends to be repeated beyond Fairtrade into other markets and projects addressing other ethical issues. In another manifestation of the general concern over the reliability of surveys in this space (Section 9.9), it is not uncommon to hear ethical producers complaining that they are having trouble getting people to pay even this amount of premium in the real world.

Of course, the trouble with reality where the majority of buyers won't pay more than 10% to solve an ethical problem is that if the externalities you are trying to address actually cost more than that to fix, then the approach needs some other intervention (usually regulatory). This is discussed further below in Section 10.2.

9.4.2 Some ethical products cost more than this to produce

Organic chicken is a good example of a standard set up by campaigners around a set of fundamental principles rather than worrying about the impact on price. The standard, which requires birds to have access to natural outdoor environments, organic feed, and a range of other measures, means that an organic chicken can cost up to four times more than an intensively reared creature. It has achieved a much smaller market share than some Fairtrade products. However, it does depend on how you want to measure success. Such standards, for example, can have greater campaigning and moral impacts than economic ones.

Nevertheless, it should be noted that many successful global ethical companies have been built upon products which are clearly priced above the 10% ceiling. Lush and Patagonia are two obvious cases in point. Having very high quality combined with impressive product innovation are key elements in their success.

9.4.3 Ethical products will tend to occupy the middle of price ranges

In Section 7.3.2, we learned now ethical products are not always the most expensive, "with key ethical products often in the mid range rather than the most expensive (which are usually designer or luxury brands)."

Between 2008 and 2013, Ethical Consumer did some detailed research into the relative price of ethical products across a range of UK consumer markets. Generally speaking, most markets can be broken down into three types of pricing approach:

(a)   There are deeply discounted products, such as supermarkets' 'value' ranges. Ethical products are rarely found in this price range partly because they are usually addressing some problem or externality which will create additional cost. This is not always the case though. For a couple of years, the only Marine Stewardship Council-certified fish fingers sold in the UK were, strangely enough, those in the Sainsbury's basics range.

(b) There are also luxury or designer brands which can cost sometimes ten or more times the usual price of a product. Gucci handbags and designer clothing are the most common examples of this product type. Sometimes ethical products are priced in an equivalent way to this but are rarely successful.

(c) The majority of products fall into a middle range between these two extremes. Most big consumer brands can be found in this middle range and most ethical products can be found here too.

If we think about markets which we know well, this is usually obvious. With cars, for example, one 'ethical' choice (perhaps an electric Nissan) costs around £25,000, well above the costs of the cheapest cars (Skodas or Dacias at £10,000). They are still much cheaper than a Rolls Royce (£250,000) and even a bit cheaper than the average UK car price (£28,000).

9.4.4 Campaigners often point to how other ways of innovating a business can keep pricing competitive while being fairer to producers or the environment

In the clothing sector particularly, where wages in sweatshops are infamously below the cost of living in many cases, campaigners will often calculate how much, for example, a 10% pay rise to its workers would cost a company. They will then compare this to other business decisions that the company has made – commonly, dividends to shareholders or bonuses to directors. During campaigns against Nike, for example, the huge annual fees paid to the basketball star Michael Jordon was commonly divided amongst the workers in the communications of campaigners to make this point. Jordon earned $44 million a year from Nike between 2002 and 2012.

9.5 For many big companies, ethical choices around production are more about risk management than finding a language to market a product

In Chapter 4 (4.3.1) we explained how much modern corporate social responsibility activity at multinational companies is about risk management. From a cynical perspective, it is about identifying, for example, environmental damage or worker safety problems as ethical issues before the general public find out about it. This approach is designed to stop an ethical risk becoming a financial risk in the future.

Once identified, these ethical risks can be mitigated by taking rational steps (such as joining a multi-stakeholder initiative) to address them. As we have discussed in Chapter 8, sometimes a multi-stakeholder initiative will come with a label or accreditation to attach to products (such as a Rainforest Alliance frog logo), but not always (such as the Better Cotton Initiative). The multi-stakeholder initiatives without product labels are much the clearest example of a purely risk management approach.

At least one academic commentator has noted how the rise in prominence of this risk management approach may be linked to the fact that price premiums have been declining (in the years to 2017) across certified or ethical markets.

9.5.1 *For other companies, good behaviour is more about good management than marketing a product*

From a less cynical perspective, there is a whole raft of business literature out there which argues that socially responsible business behaviour is just good management, and sometimes more economically efficient and profitable. Much of this is produced by environmental, social, and governance investors (see 10.3.1) and comes with some quite compelling statistics and evidence which are beyond the remit of this discussion. One key element of this argument is the importance of having an ethical vision to recruit good people and to motivate teams. Another element is that measuring and managing externalities is much better than pretending that they don't exist.

For such businesses, it may be possible to use ethical choices as part of a sales proposition, but will not be essential. This also echoes the idea (discussed in Section 1.8.4) that 'boasting' about a thing was not always an attractive trait.

9.5.2 *For larger companies, highlighting the ethical performance of just one product can lead to uncomfortable questions about the others*

In Section 9.2, the idea was touched on that the majority of 'sometimes ethical' people did not necessarily make connections between one ethical product they liked and other choices they could make. Nevertheless, some companies can be uncomfortable with accrediting just one product line as say Fairtrade, because people might reasonably ask 'does this mean that your other products are unfair'. This can be an additional reason for a company to choose not to market a particular product as ethical despite having adopted a more ethical approach.

In addition, for a large company, an ambitious programme to implement a new ethical management system across its entire production might take three years or more. This can mean that for the first years at least, it may choose not to use its more ethical approach in the marketing mix until the programme is complete.

9.6 Selling with prominent ethical claims can however perform important campaigning and educational functions

Having read all of the above, it would be tempting to conclude that selling products to ethical buyers is fraught with difficulty, and often best avoided. This is not the case. It is, as already explained, a vital part of moving towards new, more ethical economies.

It is important to begin with these warnings though, because the majority of mistakes by companies have been made by failing to understand these key details at the outset. Indeed, misunderstanding these key points has led to a whole branch of (academic) literature claiming that the idea of ethical consumers is a myth (see Section 9.9).

There are three compelling reasons why placing ethical stories somewhere in a marketing proposition can make sense, which we look at in this section and in Sections 9.7 and 9.8.

9.6.1 Ethical claims or stories around products can educate buyers about specific ethical issues

We note at many sections elsewhere how there is a rise in the idea that businesses should be able to serve other purposes as well as profitability. If, for example, a business of this type is concerned about climate change, then telling consumers that it has made a low-energy kettle serves a double function. It says, here is a great kettle which will make your tea, but it also says that addressing energy consumption in kettle design can help us collectively address a problem called climate change. This will perform a campaigning or educative function for consumers who have not thought about this particular problem before.

We also noted in Sections 7.4.3 and 3.4.3 how, for campaigners wanting to influence markets, sometimes launching a product which points the way to a solution (such as the Greenpeace Greenfreeze fridge) can be a way of making change happen. Obviously, this is also an educational project for which ethical production choices need to take centre stage.

9.6.2 It is possible to argue that producers have a responsibility to educate purchasers about the ethical issues they face

Producers, at least those with their eyes open, are much more likely than buyers to know about ethical concerns in their supply chains because they are closer to them and work with them every day. In Section 1.8, we discussed how communicating the ethical choices that are being made is also important to drive change further. In addition, a general theme of this book (10.5) is that to make markets function more ethically requires a cultural change to a situation where discussion of ethical issues in buying choices is common and everyday or 'self-conscious'. If producers know about a problem and are addressing it (perhaps collectively), but know that some of their competitors might not be, a key part of driving change will be to talk about it – in order to inform and educate buyers. They will also be contributing to the wider goal of trying to make markets generally function in a more ethical way.

9.6.3 Playing a role in the formal education system is not without controversy but may be useful

In Section 6.6.2, we discussed how educating consumers particularly about ethical buying would be good for governments to do. The Fairtrade Foundation and Fairtrade companies, for example, have also developed educational packs for schools. These packs don't take the form of sales messages for particular products, but talk more generally about poverty in agricultural sectors and the history of colonialism. This has not been without criticism, because other corporate educational materials in more controversial areas, such as those produced by the nuclear power industry, have rightly been criticised.

It is better if companies are not operating in this space, because selling to children in schools is wrong. However, if it is important for children to know about ethical issues in markets and (as in other areas) our somewhat imperfect governments are failing to provide this, then working with others to fill this gap can be useful. Because of the sensitive nature of operating in this space, it will only really work with those 'consensual' ethical areas discussed in Section 1.1.3.

9.7 In competitive markets an innovative ethical approach can become a differentiator

(a)   *In busy consumer markets*

In modern Western consumer markets, there is a profusion of choice. If I want to buy a shirt, I can go into a shop in the high street and look at perhaps 30 or 40 different types. If I go into the shop next door, there will be another 40 and so on. As discussed earlier, there are some that will be unfeasibly cheap and others that are unbelievably expensive. Most though will occupy the middle ground at what it costs to make a shirt with some mark-up for everyone else along the way. Although, as we know, consumers are only usually interested in ethics as a third factor, once price and quality have been taken into account, this is exactly the kind of factor that people need to help make a choice when such a profusion of choice exists. This is probably one of the core reasons why ethics continues to be a subject of interest to consumers, despite the difficulties in applying it, and some generally negative reflection on the phenomenon itself.

(b)   *In ethical markets*

We also saw in Section 1.3.4, how in some markets like tea in the UK ethically certified products take a majority market share. Particularly for smaller companies or new entrants, it can be difficult to signal difference. These have led to the appearance of double certified (Fairtrade and Organic) and even triple certified (Fairtrade, Organic, and Rainforest Alliance) teas and coffees. It has also led to a wide range of independent initiatives such as 'direct trade' with particular named communities (see Section 9.8). Other innovative approaches include Equal Exchange's 'grown by women' coffees trialled in 2013 in the UK.

In Sections 7.8 and 10.8.2, where we discuss competing on ethics, we note how major food retailers have been seen to use ethics in their marketing competitively. Food retail in the UK is well known as a highly competitive market.

9.8 Telling a product's story can be a useful way of engaging customers and staff

In Section 4.7.3, we looked at how some companies were making a virtue out of transparency and using it to tell a product's story to customers. The Swedish jeans producer Nudie and the US coffee company Counter Culture Coffee, which both published detailed information about their suppliers, were given as examples.

The idea of 'direct trade' initially emerged to innovate in coffee supply chains to improve on the approaches of some of the bigger certification schemes. It involves the roaster or manufacturer buying directly from the farmer rather than purchasing coffee as a commodity from a trader. Direct trading was practised by several companies in 2018, including Cafédirect, Illy Group, Solino, and Union Hand Roasted. Buyers will visit producers regularly, allowing them to build long-term relationships as well as to develop a pretty good idea of any ethical problems and virtues at the production end.

As well as bringing product quality advantages, this approach to trade, which avoids commodity markets, also allows sellers to tell stories about their suppliers to give colour and interest to an offering. Although rarely effective at point of sale, because a story is not always a simple thing to communicate, these approaches can be useful to build long-term relationships with customers, and indeed staff, making them more 'sticky' and loyal to a brand. The role of ethical business approaches generally in making stakeholders more loyal to a brand is discussed extensively elsewhere in business management literature.

There have also been many attempts to use new technologies to tell stories about product origins. These range from QR-code scanners at Mid-Counties Co-op to supply mapping projects for Fairtrade Chilean wine. None to date have really flown, but it is probably only a matter of time.

Of course, it is possible to get this approach wrong too. Tesco were publicly pilloried for creating 'fake farm' names for their budget range in

2017, in an attempt to persuade consumers of an authenticity that was not there. There is some crossover here with the discussions on transparency elsewhere in the book and in 4.7.3 particularly.

9.9 Academics talk about an 'attitude behaviour gap' which suggests that people buy fewer ethical products than they tell people in surveys

Quite early on in the development of ethical purchasing, companies launching new ethical products found that 70% of people in surveys who said they were (sometimes) interested in ethical products were not buying them. For some academics, this reinforced their preconceptions that all people were essentially self-interested and lied in consumer surveys which were not to be trusted. Some touted this as an argument that the ethical consumer was a myth and the idea of an economy where responsible purchasing was the norm was doomed.

There is evidence in surveys generally that some people do tend to give answers which shows them in a better light as people or which they think the questioner will want to hear. It has been identified in voting intention surveys, where preference for liberal or social parties can be overstated because openly supporting selfish interests can look less good. Academics call it 'social desirability bias'.

However, when we look at the distance between words and deeds in ethical buying surveys, it begins to look less likely that flaws in survey methodology are the sole cause and more likely that there must be other explanations too. In most ethical markets, we find 70% of people saying they'd like to buy ethical stuff and around a 5% market share for ethical products. If all survey results were out by a margin of 65%, there would be very few polling companies still trading rather than the giant global industry we can see today. In around 2016, when voting intention polls began to fail to predict election outcomes in the UK and USA by a margin they had not seen before, and which was the cause of much soul-searching in the industry, the margins for error were still well below 10%.

What appears to be happening in the field of ethical purchasing is a misunderstanding of the complexity of including ethics in purchasing intentions, which are also affected by a wide range of other factors. In Section 2.9.2, we considered three other possible explanations:

(a)   No alternative ethical products are available in many markets;

(b)   Some markets have ethical alternatives but they may be very expensive, or less effective, or hard to get hold of, or possibly all three; and

(c)   No campaigns have been launched to raise awareness of product problems and which ask for participation.

As was suggested in Section 2, this suggests that growing ethical markets to scale could be as much a 'supply side problem' as it is one of addressing demand.

This is further evidenced by the study of UK ethical markets discussed above (9.1(a)), which identified the involvement of big multinationals as key to big changes in market share. It was also noted, in Section 6, how government incentivisation in ethical markets could be transformative. Finally, we also noted in Section 1.3.4 that in some 'mature ethical markets' (where ethics have been discussed for more than 20 years now), certified products were taking a majority market share. This shows that it is possible for the 70% of 'sometimes ethicals' to be buying ethically all of the time, whether consciously or not.

References and notes

9.1   (a) J.G. Carrier and P. Luetchford (2012) Ethical Consumption: Social Value and Economic Practice.

Tate and Lyle (February 2008) Press Release; www.tateandlyle.com/news/tate-lyle-establishes-fairtrade-all;

https://uk.reuters.com/article/uk-tea-unilever-sustainable/unilever-to-sell-environmentally-sustainable-tea-idUKN2548375920070525

9.2   An archive of surveys of ethical consumer behaviour is maintained and published on the Ethical Consumer website in its research hub. It is summarised in the chart of consumer opinion. It also has details of surveys looking at Brazil and China.

9.2.1   (c) Marks and Spencer plc polling and research has shown this local global split. Conversation between the Author and its Sustainability team in 2019.

(d) Rise in veganism. See *Ethical Consumer Magazine*. Issue 177. March 1019. Editorial at page 3.

9.3.1   Personal communication with the author 2002. The research leading to the insight of putting less ethics into the marketing mix was the work of Simon Williams, the then marketing manager at Co-operative Bank. This has not to my knowledge been widely reported in print.

9.4.1 Fair Trade 10%: Personal communication with the author 1993.

See also Kendall Cox Park (2018) Understanding ethical consumers: Willingness-to-pay by moral cause. *Journal of Consumer Marketing*, 35(2), pp. 157–168; https://doi.org/10.1108/JCM-02-2017-2103

Price premiums declining across certified markets; see e.g. Terry Tudor (2017); https://mypad.northampton.ac.uk/cceg/tag/rainforest-alliance/#.XFcOtc3grIU

9.4.2 Price of organic chicken; see 8.2.2.1.

Organic standards; see e.g. https://www.soilassociation.org/organic-living/why-organic/better-for-animals/poultry-chickens/

9.4.3 7.3.2 *Ethical Consumer Magazine* 179 (November/December 2010) The Price of Ethics

9.4.4 https://sourcingjournal.com/topics/labor/garment-workers-living-wage-supply-chain-74069/

A. Fanshawe, L. Dufresne, F. Nicholson, J. Perkins, O. Cator and C. Beere (2017) Cicih Sukaesih's North America Nike tour. followthethings.com/cicihsukaesih.shtml;

https://www.forbes.com/sites/mattconnolly/2016/05/19/despite-lebron-james-1-billion-deal-michael-jordan-still-king-nike/#45a9c4d9cd0b

9.5 Price premiums declining across certified markets; see e.g. Terry Tudor (2017) https://mypad.northampton.ac.uk/cceg/tag/rainforest-alliance/#.XFcOtc3grIU

9.5.1 Archie B. Carroll and Kareem M. Shabana (2010) The business case for corporate social responsibility: A review of concepts, research and practice; https://onlinelibrary.wiley.com/doi/abs/10.1111/j.1468-2370.2009.00275.x

Robert G. Eccles, Ioannis Ioannou, George Serafeim (2014) The Impact of Corporate Sustainability on Organizational Processes and Performance. *Management Science*, 60(11), pp. 2835–2857.

Mercedes Rodriguez-Fernandez (2016) Social responsibility and financial performance: The role of good corporate governance. *BRQ Business Research Quarterly*, 19(2), April–June 2016, pp. 137–151.

NBS (2013) www.nbs.net/articles/three-reasons-job-seekers-prefer-sustainable-companies

9.6 Devinney, Auger and Eckhardt (2010) The Myth of the Ethical Consumer.

9.6.1.3 *Ethical Consumer Magazine*. Issue 42. July 1995. Companies in the Classroom. P. 23.

9.7 (b) See e.g. www.ethicalconsumer.org/food-drink/shopping-guide/tea and www.ethicalconsumer.org/food-drink/shopping-guide/coffee-and-coffee-beans

9.8 Direct trade; see www.ethicalconsumer.org/food-drink/shopping-guide/ coffee-and-coffee-beans

For customer loyalty and ethics, see e.g. Anne Bahr Thompson (2018) *Do Good: Embracing Brand Citizenship for Fuel Both Purpose and Profit.* AMACOM. New York;

www.thegrocer.co.uk/sourcing/midcounties-co-op-to-give-shoppers-full-ingredient-provenance/590687.article

Dorothea Kleine (2008) Negotiating partnerships, understanding power: Doing action research on Chilean Fairtrade wine value chains. *The Geographical Journal*, 174(2), Value chains and the geographies of wine production and consumption (June 2008), pp. 109–123;

www.theguardian.com/environment/2017/dec/13/tesco-faces-legal-threat-over-marketing-its-food-with-fake-farm-names

9.9 For discussions of social desirability bias and attitude behaviour gaps, see Harrison, Newholm and Shaw (2005) *The Ethical Consumer.* Sage. London.

Also Devinney, Auger and Eckhardt (2010) *The Myth of the Ethical Consumer.*

10

THEORETICAL PRINCIPLES OR WHY IT'S IMPORTANT

10.1 Failing to deal with the problem of 'externalities' is creating an existential threat for people and ecosystems

10.1.1 Economics has a notion it calls 'externalities'

Even for the high priests of neoliberalism, there are some circumstances where they have to admit that markets are not very helpful. They call these instances 'market failure' and there are some well-known phenomena, such as abuse of monopoly power, where economists admit that governments need to become involved to correct the problem. Externalities are other well-recognised types of market failure. An externality is something that happens to someone or something else when a transaction takes place which is not affected in the market price. One classic negative externality is pollution of a river. If my factory has an effluent pipe into a river, the river will not charge me any more if I put 2 kg or 2 tonnes of poison into it. This means that, unless corrected, the incentives are for me to pollute more rather than less (if it costs me money to dispose of it another way).

DOI: 10.4324/9781003200185-10

10.1.2 *Externalities historically have been addressed by governments regulating markets*

In Section 6.9, we saw how one of the key roles of governments is to provide regulatory solutions to the problem of externalising social and environmental costs. In the case of river pollution, the UK government bans some chemicals and issues 'discharge consents' for others, which limit the amount of a particular chemical that a particular company can release into a particular river over a particular time. It may then have a series of fines which it can impose if these consents are exceeded.

10.1.3 *Globalisation, the power of multinational corporations, and regulatory capture are now making some regulation more difficult*

Of course, governments have shown bias towards private commercial interests throughout history – from the East India Company to ITT in Chile. However, another key theme in this book is that the wider post-war globalisation of markets combined with 'regulatory capture' has meant that much formerly national regulation has become less easy to enforce (see 1.4.2).

Sometimes the pressure on regulators takes three forms: lobbying, persuasion, and legal threats. Sometimes it is clearly bribery and corruption. At other times, it is the quasi-corruption of the 'revolving door' between governments and business whereby friendly regulators can be rewarded with well-paid positions later. Much has been written about this elsewhere, but two classic texts are Greider's 1992 study of US democracy called 'Who will tell the people'? and Monbiot's UK analysis in 2000 called 'Captive State'.

This now occurs, to some degree, in almost every market you can observe. Like systemic tax avoidance, it has become normalised that it is acceptable behaviour for corporations to lobby in their own short-term commercial interests whatever the effect on 'external' parties. The effect of farming lobbyists on water pollution regulations in Trump era America in 2018 has provided just one example of how commercial interests can operate to weaken river pollution regulation particularly.

The same lobby's success in resisting regulation of the routine use of antibiotics in intensive animal farming is now recognised to be a key contributor to the growing problem of antibiotic resistance. It is illuminating in this case that short-term commercial interests were noted, by the corporations concerned, to be of greater importance than the long-term health prospects for the whole species globally.

10.1.4 *In its most extreme form, regulatory capture has tried to formalise itself within international trade rules*

Trade treaties, negotiated between states or trading blocks, have proven a fruitful area for corporate lobbyists to raise the commercial interests of their clients. The World Trade Organisation (WTO) is an international organisation designed to arbitrate disputes between trading nations.

It became clear during the 1990s that common sense was under threat from commercial interests within international trade law when General Agreement on Tariffs and Trade/WTO began to make rulings that government regulations on 'non-financial matters' which affected trading partners were illegal. One classic case occurred when the US government attempted to ban the import of tuna caught by nets which also caught thousands of dolphins and were told that they could not do so. The implications that governments could no longer regulate to uphold ethical standards across whole areas were alarming and proven true by later rulings.

Huge civil society demonstrations outside a WTO meeting which ended in rioting in Seattle in 1999 showed that not everyone was going to take this kind of dismantling of regulation lying down, despite its mind-boggling complexity. Since then, there has been some support for environmental standards in the WTO, but the problems of lobbying for naked self-interest at giant corporations remain. From 2010, multinational companies began to press for new trade treaties (Transatlantic Trade and Investment Partnership (TTIP) and Trans-Pacific Partnership (TPP)) which would establish 'corporate courts' with the power to rule that national government regulations were illegal.

10.1.5 *Unregulated markets can reward companies which maximise the most externalities and encourage governments to dismantle regulation*

Of course, the reason why economists agree that a regulator is necessary in the case of externalities is that, as we saw with river pollution, without it the incentives are all wrong. A company which does the right thing and builds an expensive chemical removal system into its effluent pipe will have to charge more for its product and may then fail against competitors which continue to pollute.

Campaigners in a range of different areas have dubbed this type of problem "a race to the bottom."

This tends to be used in two ways: as a race for companies and a different one for governments.

(a)　*A race to the bottom for companies*

Although this can occur in any market where the externalities are not regulated, it obviously occurred in the widespread outsourcing of manufacture from economies in the Global North to low wage/ low regulation economies in the Global South in the 1970s and the 1980s. During this period, long-established manufacturers in Europe and the USA began to move production to some Asian economies where wages were lower and other workers' protections were less good. This allowed them to price their products lower than companies which had not yet moved, forcing the latter to have to consider following suit or failing to compete. Whole industries, clothing and footwear particularly, ended up relocating.

(b)　*A race to the bottom for governments*

To compete for the business of multinationals, governments may be keen to limit their own regulation. With much of the outsourcing of manufacture discussed above going to China, there is some evidence that governments in Bangladesh and Vietnam were keen to keep regulation and wages even lower than those in China in order to try to compete for the attention of manufacturers.

Perhaps an even clearer example of a race to the bottom in regulation has been reduction in corporation tax rates across the world, now well documented by the Organisation for Economic Co-operation and Development (OECD) and others.

10.1.6 Externalities are not a minor issue but a whole system problem which damages ecosystems, human rights, and animal welfare

It is not new to see externalities as problematic. Marx, for example, saw them as one of many fundamental flaws in capitalism in the 1870s – but before the language of 'externality' was used. However, the reach and effectiveness of systematic pressure by commercial interests in the neoliberal global economy has seen a reversal in the long trend for improving social standards which had taken place following the industrial revolution.

Nicholas Stern, in his 2006 report for the UK government on climate change, saw carbon emissions as a clear case of an externality inadequately regulated in the face of an obvious market failure. The role and effectiveness of corporate lobbies for coal and oil industries during the Conference of the Parties (COP) sequence of international climate negotiations is now extensively documented.

Externalities started out in this discussion as a technical example of market failure easily corrected by regulation but have reached the point where, with climate change particularly and widespread corporate capture of regulators, they have become a widely acknowledged existential threat to the future of the human (and other) species.

10.2 Ethical purchasing can provide an additional corrective mechanism for the tendency of markets to reward companies which maximise their externalities

The first point to make is that while ethical purchasing campaigns are often concerned with bringing social and environmental 'externalities' into the cost of a product, not all ethical purchasing is about trying to fix the race to the bottom. As discussed elsewhere, some boycotts are about expressing moral disapproval of particular actions. Other approaches, like some choices around veganism and buying electric cars, are about challenging the bigger system within which decisions are made. However much ethical buying and selling, particularly where ethical labels and standards are concerned, is very much about addressing the problem of externalities. As discussed above, some of these, like the Fairtrade (food) and the Forest Stewardship Council (forestry) and the Marine Stewardship Council (fishing) labels, have gone on to make significant impacts on some global markets. However, much of the political tension around such labels, also discussed extensively elsewhere, arises when the costs of a particular intervention are high.

10.2.1 Problems may arise when the cost of fixing a particular externality exceeds any additional amount the majority of purchasers are willing to pay

As already discussed under selling to ethical purchasers (9.4.1):

> the trouble with a reality where the majority of buyers won't pay more than 10% to solve an ethical problem is that, if the externalities you are

trying to address actually cost more than that to fix, then the approach needs some other intervention.

The first point to make is that this 10% 'ceiling' is mainly found in consumer markets. Where key purchasers are in governments, local authorities, or charities, they are not always seeking a competitive price above all else in the usual way.

The second point to make is that fixing ethical problems do not always come at a noticeable cost. Energy efficiency measures, for example, which usually end up saving money, are the classic examples in this case.

We also saw in selling to ethical purchasers (Chapter 9) that the cost of fixing some ethical problems was sufficiently small for the producer to be able to absorb it without passing the costs on. This arguably occurs in the UK with some Fairtrade products.

However, where these exceptions do not apply, and as discussed in previous chapters, there are two types of intervention which can be observed contributing to viable and successful ethical alternatives. The first is government intervention and the second is industry collaborations.

10.2.2 If markets work more efficiently when ethical purchasing occurs, then it makes sense for governments to both pursue and encourage ethical purchasing

Chapter 6 is dedicated to the various interventions that governments can and do make around ethical purchasing. At 6.2 (a) it was noted that

> is likely to be economically inefficient for society to absorb social and environmental costs after the event. For example, it may be better for public sector organisations to buy exclusively renewable energy now, rather than pay for the costs of addressing flood damage later on.

Another example came to public attention in the UK when it emerged that wages were so low at some mainstream supermarket chains (including Tesco and Asda, the biggest food companies in the country) that some workers were having to claim welfare benefits to make ends meet. Consumer desire for cheap products and investor desire for high returns meant that downward pressure on wages was a consequence whose external effects were being shared collectively by the state.

The Living Wage Campaign had already emerged in 2001 as a civil society accreditation mechanism (or ethical labelling scheme) for companies paying workers at a reasonable level. In the face of these and other revelations, the government made dramatic increases to the minimum wage laws in 2016 – although still to a level below that set by the Living Wage Campaign.

It therefore can be said that it makes sense (in mainstream economic terms) for governments to either regulate to address externalities or to encourage ethical purchasing in order to:

(a)   reduce public costs, and
(b)   make markets better reflect the real cost of what they do, and
(c)   help markets to work better with 'perfect information'.

Very specifically, around the problem of externalities and willingness to pay extra, governments can also use tax or fiscal arrangements to try to compensate for the higher prices of some ethical products. This was discussed in Section 6.7, where the example of electric car subsidies was used, and it was noted how it appeared to be an underexplored area of regulatory intervention.

Of course, in a kind of catch-22 scenario, these ethical purchasing interventions by governments can also be affected by the power of corporate lobbying. However, they do have some advantages in this regard. First, it is easier to make national rather than global level interventions of this type. The UK government cannot ban child labour in Pakistan, but it can support the Fairtrade movement financially through its Development Aid budget. Second, where large groups of certified producers develop, it can split the corporate lobby with at least some economically powerful voices arguing for ethical interventions.

It is also in some sense 'fairer' if externalities are 'internalised' into the cost of a product. The people who are benefiting from avoiding the true cost of a product (e.g. car drivers and pollution) are not always the people (children living by road) who suffer from an externality.

10.2.3 Cross-industry collaborations can also address the race to the bottom problem to some degree

Earlier chapters have introduced the idea of multi-stakeholder initiatives or industry collaborations set up to address particular ethical problems. If we put aside for the moment the ones which are obviously just window dressing to demonstrate fake concern, there are some which have been able to offer genuine evidence of impact. The Better Cotton Initiative, for example (8.1.4), was set up to address both environmental and labour issues in the cotton supply chain and includes some of the clothing sector's biggest players. The Bangladesh Fire and Safety Accord was another garment sector initiative set up by campaigners and trade unions to establish minimum health and safety standards in Bangladesh following the Rana Plaza disaster in 2015 (where more than 1,000 workers were killed when a multistorey factory collapsed). Again, the majority of key industry players either joined voluntarily or were publicly shamed until they did.

The subtext to this kind of approach is that if the bulk of your competitors agree that the problem needs solving too and everyone is solving it at the same time in the same way, then poor worker safety, for example, will cease to become a competitiveness issue and there will be no race-to-the-bottom competition from others who think that worker deaths are fine.

The problem with this approach is that in more developed economies particularly, there are very powerful laws to prevent companies colluding to raise prices to increase profits. These anti-trust rules have been set up to address a very real and long-standing problem in free markets. Because of this, companies can be wary of even entering a room with competitors for fear of unusually rigorous enforcement rules, including prison sentences. It is clear that traditional economic thinking is again (see below) behind the pace when it comes to addressing real world problems of this type. To define consumer interest purely as a short-term concern, with low prices rather than a more complex issue where long-term interests in sustainability and social justice are important too, shows the degree to which traditional economic thinking needs to move ahead (10.8). The Fairtrade Foundation published some detailed research on this subject in 2019 when it became clear that this was a barrier to addressing a wide range of issues including child labour in the cocoa industry. They argued that there is an obvious need for regulators everywhere to make very clear that collaboration to address sustainability and social justice issues is good.

10.2.4 The US campaigner Cesar Chavez described consumer actions addressing the race to the bottom as capitalism in reverse

In the 1960s California, poor wages and working conditions in agriculture meant that average life expectancy was 49 years for migrant workers.

One of the workers Cesar Chavez began a drive to unionise the workforce and, helped by others, established the United Farm Workers (UFW) union. Chavez became internationally famous because he realised that there may be sympathy for his cause further up the supply chain – amongst ordinary consumers. Much of their produce was sold in the traditionally liberal North Western cities where sympathy for social injustices was more common. His campaign grew to become known as the then famous California Grape Boycott and gathered support from a broad coalition of church groups, other trade unions, Non-Governmental Organisations (NGOs), consumer organisations, and mainstream journalists. This coalition joined picket lines and marches, signed petitions, supported labour laws, lobbied elected officials, distributed educational flyers, produced documentaries, penned songs, performed plays, held teach-ins, and generally supported the nationwide boycott.

The farmers were not easily moved. However, by 1969, sales of Californian grapes in New York were down by 30%, and by 1970 the majority of the farmers had signed recognition agreements with the UFW, significant improvements had been made in wages and working conditions, and the boycott was called off. The five-year-long boycott is now recognised as one of the most successful in US history, and Chavez – delighted on hearing of its success – is recorded as exclaiming that this was surely 'capitalism in reverse'.

He died, celebrated, in April 1993, and so it is no longer possible to enquire into what he actually meant by this. But the idea that purchaser pressure operating in markets can lead to an improvement in standards rather than simply a constant pressure for lower prices must have been part of what he was trying to articulate.

10.3 Ethical purchasing can be seen as part of a wider movement calling for a consciously ethical approach to all economic transactions

Ethical purchasing occurs because people are asking questions about the ethical consequences of some of their economic transactions. Commonly, one question is "am I contributing financially to activities with which I disagree?" It is also possible to observe other organisations asking similar ethical questions about other economic choices such as investment, lending, selling, hiring, and employment. Although it is not a pretty phrase, we could call it 'transactional ethicism' to be going along with. The notion of transactional ethicism allows us to articulate the idea of a wider movement calling for a consciously ethical approach to all economic transactions. We will look at the three main types in the next three subsections, and will then look at some of the characteristics of this movement in Sections 10.4 and 10.5.

10.3.1 *Ethical investment and lending*

The idea of ethical investment has been around for a least as long as the idea of ethical purchasing. Confusingly perhaps, it has also become known as Socially Responsible Investment, Environmental, Social, and Governance investment, Sustainability Investment, and more recently, Impact Investment. In the same way as ethical purchasing, its origins lay in institutions ostensibly concerned with ethics being targeted by civil society campaigners asking them to justify ethically what they were doing. Key moments in the modern ethical investment movement included campaigners asking Churches about their investments in the 1970s apartheid South Africa and also about their investments in companies manufacturing chemical weapons for use in the Vietnam War. The targeting of investors is also discussed in the Campaigning chapter in Section 7.6.3. The similar tactic of targeting banks over unethical lending is covered there too (in Section 7.6.2).

Ethical Investment has now grown to the stage where some of its ideas are being applied, according to some measures, to around 50% of all European and 25% of all US investments. For those whom this means anything, this was measured to be worth $30.7 trillion in assets in 2018.

We have seen in other chapters how ethical investors have contributed to the pressure for corporate social responsibility reporting within multinational companies (4.3.1), how Local Authorities can be important ethical investors (5.1), and in Chapter 3 and elsewhere, how purchasing campaigns can work in parallel with ethical investor groups to aggregate the pressure for change across a range of issues.

Like ethical purchasing, the depth of impact on major corporations of the ethical investment movement has been questioned. What is clear is that positive investment in smaller companies can have a much more easily measurable effect, and it has not been insignificant.

The Ethical Investment movement has spawned a great many books looking in detail at its practices, theories, and impacts, so it is not necessary to cover it further here.

10.3.2 Ethical selling

This is not the same as selling ethical products, which is covered in Chapter 9, but specifically addresses how the seller speaks to the consumer or purchaser ethically and encompasses the sale of problem or damaging products such as tobacco. The Co-operative Bank in the UK used the language of big ethics and small ethics to illustrate this distinction internally in the 1990s. Big ethics were for the global social and environmental impacts of lending decisions, whereas small ethics were for the way the customer was treated.

This tends to be a much more closely regulated area of corporate behaviour, as states had long ago discovered that unregulated corporations may, with inexplicable short-sightedness, wantonly injure their own customers if not restrained. A well-known case of regulatory failure occurred in China in 2008, when it was discovered that milk and infant formula products were being adulterated by a wide range of companies with the industrial chemical melamine. In the EU, consumer protection laws are pretty comprehensive, but there are still areas where the failure to exercise ethical judgement has become controversial.

A useful case by way of illustrating a number of recurring factors in this book is the use of red, yellow, and green traffic light labels on food products to show high salt, fat, and sugar content. Since 2013, public health campaigners have held that they would be a useful way to help rising levels of obesity in Europe. However, lobbying from food multinationals, particularly Kellogg's and other breakfast cereal companies, have kept these regulations 'voluntary' for nearly ten years.

Examining ethical issues in selling can also extend beyond selling safe products and telling the truth about them. The rise of concern over hate speech and fake news globally in 2016 also let campaigners to ask companies to examine whether they had been contributing to the problem by buying adverts for their products in media which were promoting this kind of agenda. Campaigns against Breitbart in the USA and the Stop Funding Hate campaign in the UK made a significant impact in this space.

The idea of ethical selling also means that, in theory, you can unethically sell an ethical product. The Co-op Bank in the UK, despite its big and small ideas discussed above, was fined in 2017 (along with many other UK banks) for mis-selling unsuitable insurance products to its customers.

10.3.3 *Ethical employment*

This transaction has people asking ethical questions from both sides.

For people seeking to employ someone, there are commonly both regulatory criteria to try to prevent the worst types of unethical hiring practices. In the UK, for example, it is against the law to treat someone less favourably than someone else in a hiring process because of a personal characteristic such as religion, sex, gender reassignment, or age. We also saw in Chapter 6 on ethical purchasing by governments that affirmative action programmes in the USA to encourage employment of ethnic minorities (driven by purchasing) have also been quite significant historically (6.3.1).

On top of legal rules are a range of desirable ethical employment criteria or rights around how to treat people once they are employed. Some of these have now been codified in places like the International Labour Organisation (ILO) treaties and the Ethical Trading Initiative (ETI) 'base code' and in national laws too. These include issues like non-discrimination, a living wage, and freedom to join trade unions. The role of codes in addressing workers' rights in international supply chains was discussed in more detail in Chapter 4 (in Sections 4.3 and 4.5).

On the other side, it is possible to observe reflections by employees on the ethical choices of joining a particular employer. Of course, we know from other areas of study that the majority of people can be described as 'sometimes ethical' (see Section 9.2). It would therefore be possible to assume that most people at some stage in their lives have faced difficult ethical choices around who to work for, particularly when they find that their employer has done something with which they disagree. There is lots of anecdotal evidence of this too. Like price and quality in ethical purchasing though, there are other factors in employment choices like economics and practicality which make such decisions complex.

However, although there is less self-conscious collective activity in this area, it is worth noting that these kinds of decisions, like consumer boycotts, can have a collective impact. We know for example that some controversial industries, despite high wages, find it difficult to attract the most talented staff. The *Guardian* newspaper, looking at employment in the tobacco industry in 2016 titled its report tellingly as "the problem with selling a lethal product: you just can't get the staff." We also noted in Section 1.5.2, how companies targeted by boycotts over ethical issues had identified recruitment problems too.

10.4 This movement offers a system-level solution to some of the system-level problems within modern capitalism

As we have observed earlier, much ethical market campaigning is simply looking to address current and pressing problems such as sweatshop labour in a particular industry or tax avoidance at a particular multinational (Chapter 2). The same is true of investor collaborations, like the previously mentioned carbon disclosure project (4.6.2). Campaigners and consumers involved are not always part of a self-conscious movement which feels it has a broader narrative about how to fix some of the systemic problems within modern global capitalism, or indeed within human societies more generally. However, one of the advantages of looking at all these campaigns and activities together under the umbrella notion of ethical purchasing or indeed transactional ethicism is that it is possible to argue that there is a movement here that does have some system level answers.

We have already discussed above how it is widely accepted that externalities are a system level problem within global capitalism (10.1). It is also self-evident that the underlying cause of the race to the bottom this creates in unregulated markets is what we could call 'extreme profit-seeking' or 'profit-seeking without a moral compass'. We also discussed how ethical purchasing can provide a corrective mechanism to the problem of externalities generally. It is also able to 'call out' or shame or even impact economically extreme profit-seeking in other ways (see boycotts in Chapter 2). Later on, we also discuss how promoting a new ethical language around economics is also an important part of the work that this movement does (10.5).

The argument would therefore be that if all economic actors could learn to apply an ethical filter to all their economic transactions, then actors making unethical choices to maximise their externalities would lose market share and eventually – using Marxist language – wither away.

In other words, the idea of transactional ethicism, if practised widely enough, offers a systemic solution to at least some of the systemic problems within globalised capitalism itself. In some markets, we have seen evidence of how this can work (1.3.4 and 9.7).

There are three key advantages or characteristics of this system level approach which are discussed further here: its immediacy and gradualist nature, its ability to work whether or not governing institutions support it, and its approach to reforming productive enterprises themselves.

10.4.1 *Transactional ethicism can also break reform of global capitalism down into manageable chunks and can choose its own timetables*

The notion of a 'mature ethical market', where campaigners have been working for decades and where ethical products were beginning to take a majority market share, has already been discussed above (1.3.4 and 9.7). Coffee and bananas in the UK are two commonly used examples. There are other markets, for example, golf clubs and sodium hexachloride, where examination of ethical issues has barely begun. In this sense, although transactional ethicism offers a whole system change because its method of operation can in theory work across every possible transaction, the reality is that it can be observed delivering social and environmental improvements in a gradualist way: market by market and issue by issue. Campaigners will discover a particular problem with a particular system of production and get to work inside a particular market to try to get the support of purchasers to fix it (Chapter 7).

This can be frustrating when, for many people, it is already clear what wider system changes are necessary, and that a more revolutionary system change might be possible by changing the regulator or the system itself. The idea that regulatory solutions are not easily available in globalised markets without an obvious regulatory system globally has been discussed elsewhere (1.4.2). In the face of complex issues like this, transactional ethicism has the advantage of offering an approach which can begin to drive changes within a couple of weeks while people are waiting for elections to come around or even for the proletariat to rise up.

It is perhaps most important to note that the various approaches to system change available are not mutually exclusive and can be working in parallel at the same time.

The final point to note here is that the gradualist change that can be observed does appear to be cumulative. For example, the number of fisheries which is being added to the MSC labelling is increasing over time, as are the number of food commodities for which Fairtrade standards are being worked out. Of course, there are reverses from time to time because of the political nature of this space, but by and large, the movement is one towards a gradual improvement. It is possible to envision a wave of ethical standards growing to encompass most markets over time.

10.4.2 *Transactional ethicism can function whether or not the governing institutions of the day support it*

Margaret Thatcher, a key early proponent of neoliberalism, possessed an antipathy towards social and environmental interventions and propounded a belief that unregulated markets worked best. It may be coincidence that much of the early growth and development of ethical consumer projects in the UK occurred in the 1980s during her watch. Consumer boycotts particularly, including successful ones against apartheid South Africa, chlorofluorocarbons (CFCs) in aerosols and against animal testing by cosmetics companies, all came about because it became clear to campaigners that asking the government of the day to regulate was pointless.

The notion of 'regulatory capture', whereby powerful corporations become so close to governments that governments are more likely to protect the interests of corporations rather than the interests of their citizens, is also a recurring theme in this book (Chapters 1, 5, 7, and 10). Another useful characteristic of transactional ethicism therefore is that it can offer a 'work-around' to the problem of regulatory capture in some circumstances.

A second recurring theme of this book is that ethical purchasing works much better when governments support it. There is an inherent tension between these two principles, but they can co-exist. It is simply that the most beneficial impacts of ethical purchasing may not be realised when unsympathetic regulators hold the reins of power.

Occasionally, some governments, presumably the well-captured ones, will try to regulate to prevent ethical purchasing taking place. In the chapter looking at ethical purchasing by local authorities, we looked at how this was commonly circumscribed by legal rules (5.4), occasionally even accompanied by lists of ethical issues (like trade union membership), which these types of purchasers are not allowed to take into account. Even more occasionally, there are reports of attempts to make consumer boycotts illegal. Apparently this has been the case in France and also in some US states over boycotts focussed on Israel and Palestine.

10.4.3 *Transactional ethicism appears to help reform the very institutions (firms) that operate capitalism itself*

Some of the problems of extreme profit-seeking that can be observed within capitalism can be traced back to the idea of 'shareholder primacy', which is hard-coded into the constitutions of many modern firms. This is a prevailing idea that companies, in the USA particularly, are obliged by law to maximise profits for shareholders whatever the consequences for other stakeholders. This is self-evidently a pernicious doctrine for anyone remotely near a moral compass, and its reform has attracted the attention of both regulators and campaigners for more than 20 years now.

In Chapter 1 (Basic Principles), it was stated that 'ethical purchasing is normally practised to channel economic resources towards more ethical suppliers and away from more problematic ones' (1.5). One effect of this is that it allows economic arguments to be made for social decisions. For example, when it is possible to observe some strategic discussions going on inside big corporations, the existence of ethical purchasing is useful to those promoting a more ethical approach when faced by other factions promoting a short-term profit maximisation approach.

More significantly, and as noted in Section 10.9, it can also be observed that 'the growth of ethical purchasing is also a key factor in the emergence of new mission-oriented company types' (8.6). B-Corporations, also discussed there, provide the clearest example of reform of firms taking place, since thousands of existing companies are already recorded as having converted into B-Corporation company types (whereby shareholder primacy is expressly forbidden). The B-Corporation movement cites the growth of ethical purchasing as a key driver of change.

10.4.4 Transactional ethicism is not a panacea, but it is likely to be a critical part of sustainable future

The ecological and social impacts of under-regulated global capitalism are too complex and widespread for transactional ethicism to be able to solve them quickly enough on its own. Regulatory interventions across a wide range of other issues will clearly be essential too. For example, the rising inequality caused by poor redistributional policies and compounded by technological advances like robotics means that some radical solutions like universal basic incomes currently appear to be necessary for the future to be viable for everyone. And, as discussed in principle 7.1.2 ('not every political issue can be addressed through market campaigns, but a surprising number can be'), many political problems are much more easily solved by following normal political processes. It is beyond the scope if this book to list them all here.

In addition, some markets simply don't provide ethical options for people to choose or invest in. This has been a key issue in addressing climate change through market campaigns. If there is no public transport, for example, asking people in rural areas to give up driving for ecological reasons simply does not work.

Nevertheless if the future is going to have any competitive markets operating anywhere, it is likely that an awareness of the need for ethical purchasing will play a useful role in preventing them from running too far out of control. Even when regulation is working fairly well, new developments – particularly technological ones – mean that regulating out unethical choices can run many years behind a problem emerging. This is particularly the case if the problem is a global one where co-ordinated regulation between different governments is necessary. Genetic modification of food crops was just one example of where this problem occurred, and is discussed in this context in a little more detail in Section 10.6.

In the next section, the key role of changing language in cultural change and the role of ethical purchasing in making ethical discourse easier is discussed.

Given that this power to date has largely been used to protect human rights, animal welfare, and to try to mitigate against the worst kinds of environmental damage, its growth may play a vital role in helping to create the sustainable and socially just societies which most people desire for the future.

Transactional ethicism therefore does not claim to provide a comprehensive solution to all problems, but can make an important contribution to the aggregate pressure for change in market economies across a range of key issues.

10.5 Like many movements, changing language and culture are central to how it works

Transactional ethicism involves arguing that to live in a world where markets are not unsustainable and inhumane, it is useful if purchasers and investors can learn to take ethical issues into account for most of the things they buy. On one level, it can appear that this argument is not particularly profound. Like some religions or other calls for more moral behaviour, it seems to be saying that if people all acted a bit more nicely, the world would be a nicer place.

Whilst this is true to some degree, on another level – the level of language – it is clear that transactional ethicism brings something more complex to the table. Learning to purchase ethically all the time is primarily a cultural change, and at the heart of most cultural changes are changes to the language or words we have available to describe what we do. Later on in this section, some of the new words, like organic and Fairtrade, appearing in the world of ethical purchasing are discussed. However, the moment in human history where this cultural change is occurring is important too, as it is likely to be, in many senses, a reaction against the growth of a much too narrow 'economic' thinking.

10.5.1 The dominance of the discipline of economics has led to a reduction in ethical discourse in society generally

Economics has become the dominant discipline in the modern world for both professional politicians and leaders in business and finance. And, as we discuss in more detail in the section below, economics has not covered itself in glory dealing with ethical issues. Either intentionally or from genuine confusion, the idea has emerged that there are a set of issues which are 'economic' rather than political or social or environmental or indeed ethical.

The net effect of the dominance of economics and the affirmation of selfishness that coexists within some of its essential doctrines is that the language of ethics has been eclipsed by economic language in mainstream discourse for many years. Governments measure progress as Gross Domestic Product (GDP) and adverts tell consumers what a great price their products are selling at. This would not matter so much were markets a small part of our lives. However, as we have already discussed, the rise of neoliberalism has brought with it the encroachment of markets into ever more areas of life (1.2.1). And the growth of globalised supply chains, discussed in 4.1, also means that purchasers are less able to see what's going wrong for producers on the other side of the world.

Economic language can also seek to hide or avoid ethical issues. 'Regulatory arbitrage', a particularly unfavourite phrase of mine, is described as "a practice whereby firms capitalise on loopholes in regulatory systems in order to circumvent unfavourable regulation." This could otherwise be defined as bullying countries into reducing protections for humans and the environment which are unfavourable to shareholders.

In conclusion, the growing role of markets globally, coupled with the rise of economic management ideas, has created a tendency to squeeze out ethical discourse from society. One of the key impacts of the ethical purchasing movement, as discussed throughout this book, is to reverse or at least challenge this trend.

10.5.2 *Many of the projects and collaborations around ethical purchasing are creating a new language for a new movement*

On one level, the core purpose of this book is to share an understanding of how this new language is being used. So, the many new or unfamiliar terms appearing in previous chapters constitute the beginning of a list of important ones. It would be dull to list them all again here, although it is useful to group them together into different types.

Before doing this, it is also useful to make the point that much of the language used in ethical purchasing discourse is not new. Much ethical purchasing is about addressing long-standing problems in a new way, so the problems themselves use familiar language such as workers' rights, pollution, animal welfare, conflict minerals, and modern slavery. In addition, much of the political language that helps to understand what is happening is also not new, such as race-to-the bottom, corporate capture, and neoliberalism.

The new language developing in this space around this new approach to problem-solving can be divided into five main types:

(a) *Whole system terminologies*

Perhaps the most important terms culturally are those which describe the whole movement or aspects of it. These include ethical consumption, sustainable procurement, solidarity purchasing, and green buying. Political consumption is a particularly interesting variation, which is discussed in more detail in Section 10.5.3.

(b) *Categories of campaign approaches*

There are not many of these, but because they frame the others, they are important. They include ethical boycotts, positive buying, market campaigns, and ethical rankings.

(c) *Eco-labels and multi-stakeholder initiatives*

Almost a subcategory of (b – positive buying), these are the solutions which have proliferated the most and constitute by far the largest language group. Chapter 8 explained how there were 465 specifically active eco-labels globally – each creating a new set of words to describe what it is trying to do. Some like Fairtrade and Organic are so significant as to constitute their own recognised movements.

(d) *Corporate responses*

Largely responses to the wider movement for transactional ethicism, these include expressions such as sustainability reporting and corporate social responsibility.

(e) *Technical tools*

Finally, there are a range of expressions which describe common models used to address issues in this new world: supply chain transparency, life cycle analysis, ethical purchasing policy, and whole life costing are just some of these.

10.5.3 Another key element of the cultural change is learning how to develop a critical mindset around product and service origins

When looked at over the span of human history, having any choice at all in some markets is a relatively recent phenomenon. Within living memory, in the UK any shop with chocolate or bananas or a new type of clothing would be news in a small town. Being critical of product origins in this context is then a relatively recent luxury. In addition, use of outdated libel laws by wealthy businesses to silence any critics (3.2.1) was not uncommon in the UK until at least the early 1990s. This meant that the idea of critical discourse around a product's origins was not always at the forefront of people's minds. However, the arrival of ethical boycotts in the 1980s created the idea of having a different perspective.

In the UK, stories about malpractice in supply chains are now much more common, although we have also seen that this doesn't always mean that people then infer likely problems in other markets (9.2.1). The need for formal education in schools to develop a critical mindset around all purchases has therefore also been raised as an important additional intervention that governments can make (6.6.2).

To some extent, the whole discourse around ethical consumption is about creating critical ethical thinking in markets. One group of academics (Barnett et al.) has called it 'problematizing consumption'. It is possible that, in the future, advanced cultures will be as used to the idea of product critics or indeed corporate critics as they are of film and theatre critics today.

10.5.4 Sometimes people call collective action in this space 'political consumption'

Michelle Micheletti, a professor of Political Science in Stockholm, has used the term political consumption to describe much of this kind of activity. This works particularly well when studying campaigns where there is much less agreement over what is the best ethical approach, such as the ongoing consumer boycott of Israel over its activities in Palestine (see also 1.1.2).

The notion of political consumption, it should be said, is also useful in that it can remind us that not all market campaigns are necessarily ethical. The classic case cited in this instance is the consumer boycott of Jewish businesses which the Nazi party organised in the 1930s Germany. These types of activities are still observed today with reports in 2019 of boycotts of Muslim businesses in Sri Lanka by Buddhist activists.

The crossover between ethical and political consumption is, in practice, actually very large. Indeed, any ethical consumer campaign where there is a clear set of changes that campaigners would like to see could also be described as political consumption. And the third key principle of ethical labelling scheme, noted in Section 8.3, was "Ethical labelling schemes are essentially political projects."

The preference for the term 'ethical' arises for two reasons. First, it helps the discussion to be framed around trying to find consensus by addressing the question of what constitutes ethical or socially responsible behaviour. Second, it brings into the discussion many of the more 'discrete' types of ethical purchasing behaviour, which were identified at in Section 2.5.

10.5.5 The problem of cultural appropriation is not insignificant

For people troubled by the damaging effects of capitalism, the ability of capitalist institutions to absorb and 'appropriate' the ideas of movements opposing what it does is a long-standing problem. From the punk rock movements of the 1970s to the 'cultural appropriation' by advertisers of feminist language in the early 21st century, this is well charted territory.

With ethical purchasing and selling, this problem is particularly intense, because commodification and the promotion of products are at the heart of what capitalism does. However, just as the appropriation of feminist ideas is not a reason to reject feminism, the appropriation of ethical business ideas is not a reason to reject ethical purchasing. Ethical purchasers just need to be particularly aware and on their guard for greenwash, bluewash, and all the other types of washing that occur in this space.

As we discussed in Chapter 8 and elsewhere, this problem is particularly prevalent in the field of ethical labelling schemes and positive buying. This is one reason why boycotts and name and shame campaigns will always retain a key role in the ethical purchasing movement.

On another level, part of the goals of this movement is to get the producers of goods to not just absorb the language of ethics, but to absorb core ethical values into the heart of their business models. This is covered in a little more detail in Section 10.9.

10.6 Like capitalism itself, ethical purchasing appears dynamic and capable of changing fast to address new issues

10.6.1 Ethical purchasing can usefully address ethical issues arising from technological or managerial innovations before regulations come along

What makes ethical purchasing such a useful additional tool to help address some of the damaging effects of capitalism is that it can begin campaigns and start having impacts within days or weeks of a problem emerging. This is particularly the case where technological or management innovations begin to throw up new ethical issues.

Regulation, whilst nearly always more effective, may be months or years away, particularly if it needs to happen internationally or if it is in the commercial interests of business to stall or hamper the introduction of new rules. These two factors, as discussed previously, are increasingly prevalent. The interactions between consumer campaigns and regulation which occurred when the effects of CFCs on the ozone layer became clear are instructive here (see also 6.9.1). Whilst ultimately successfully banned by targets set in an international agreement in 1989, consumer boycotts in the UK had managed to persuade manufacturers to remove them from aerosols, which constituted 60% of market use at that time, before the regulations became effective (10.6.4).

In the same way, we can observe ethical market campaigns changing over time as new issues arise or old ones are solved. Purchasers in the 1970s were concerned about racism in South Africa in campaigns that are just a memory now. Palm Oil's links to habitat destruction became a central concern to purchasers in the second decade of the 21st century, as its popularity as an ingredient expanded enormously.

And in the future, it is clear that the new technologies of Robotics and AI, particularly in the hands of profit-seeking corporations, are going to throw up many difficult ethical issues. It is almost certain that the civil society market campaigns of the future will be engaged in trying to introduce some kind of moral framework around the developments that occur.

10.6.2 *Ethical purchasing can remain an important political tool even if markets become more local*

At the time of writing (2019), the idea of a retreat from globalisation in Western democracies is high on the agenda. In theory, such a move is also compatible with an ethical future, although with its main cheerleaders being the racist right embodied by Trump, Brexit, and Salvi, the direction of travel for ethics does not look promising.

If our markets were to become simpler and less globalised, then in theory governments can regulate away more of the externalities without the problem of uncompetitiveness. This has however been the opposite of the deregulatory agenda promoted by current far-right discourse. We also know that even when governments can regulate, they may operate in corrupt or self-serving ways and choose not to do so. There are also emerging or new problems, such as AI and robotics discussed above, where governments and campaigners may not see eye to eye on the need for regulation. In all these circumstances, progressive purchasing can remain an important way to oppose corporate abuse within national boundaries.

There are also instructive lessons from the past in how consumer boycotts can play an important role in ostracising more extreme political views when they are connected to trade and commerce locally. The word boycott itself originated in an 1880s campaign of ostracism operated locally in county Mayo in Ireland against a land agent called Captain Boycott who was evicting poorer tenants.

And during the South Africa boycott, we know that a boycott of white-owned shops by poor black customers in the Eastern Cape and elsewhere led the shops to pressure the government to repeal an act (the Separate Amenities Act) that had caused the boycotts in the first place.

Finally, it is worth noting that the principle in Section 7.1.2 said that "Not every political issue can be addressed through market campaigns, but a surprising number can be." It provided further examples such as Stop

Funding Hate's UK campaign to pressure advertisers to stop advertising in UK newspapers with openly racist agendas.

10.6.3 Until we have effective democratic global governance, ethical buying may have to be a key element in having globalised markets which are not too destructive to be viable

One solution to the problem of the tendency for ethical standards to race to the bottom (10.1) in globalised markets is to have effective democratic global governance. There is a system of international law, and having specific treaties to address specific market problems arranged between sovereign states has been shown to be effective in the case of CFCs and the Montreal protocol (see 6.9.4). Other examples though are less easily forthcoming, and one-off treaties appear to be a cumbersome approach to what is after all a systemic problem which needs lots of these kind of agreements. More than a few commentators have spotted that a global regulator for global markets would be a useful thing to have, and there is some debate whether reformed UN institutions could carry out this role. However, until such reforms are forthcoming, if markets are to remain global, it looks like ethical purchasing will continue to play a key role in creating ethical frameworks to help out in this space.

Incidentally, other commentators have noted that global governance would also be useful in addressing other types of market failure which are having a detrimental effect on humans. Monopoly regulation on a global level, for example, is another key economic intervention that is long overdue.

The role of lobbying by multinational companies to prevent the emergence of this type of regulatory framework is probably not inconsequential, and is surely the subject of useful additional research.

10.7 Ethical purchasing poses interesting questions regarding the nature of democracy and participation

10.7.1 Left and right tend to respond differently to the issue of purchasing and democracy

Under basic principles (in 1.6.4), it was stated that ethical purchasing was a power which has been likened to voting or democratic power. It was also noted how this was problematic for some commentators (mainly on the left) because rich people could be seen as having a greater vote, and was a reason to prefer electoral democracy whenever this is possible.

For some on the right, the existence of ethical purchasing has been used as an argument for capitalism or at least market-based solutions. If the majority of people buy, for example, cheap food without a care for the welfare of animals and humans in the supply chain, they argue that this means that a fair and democratic way to decide on priorities has given this outcome. In Section 9.9, it was noted that a similar argument usually fails to ask whether any real, affordable choice was offered to people in the first place or indeed whether people had any information about what was happening upon which to act.

Both of these views offer interesting points and have been debated extensively elsewhere, but neither view makes cogent arguments for not purchasing ethically when possible.

There are however three other principles worth understanding in this area.

10.7.2 Viewing purchasing as a vote allows important reflection on the nature of 'abstention'

As already discussed, in the context of ethical purchasing, and often just in purchasing generally, many commentators have likened the act of purchase as a vote. This is useful in the field of ethical purchasing in one sense because it can bring to light the essentially political nature (and potential power) of each purchase.

In Section 1.3.4 and elsewhere, we have discussed survey data which revealed that around 30% of people were not interested in purchasing ethically and that around 60% only purchased ethically some of the time. It is likely that a similar number of institutions also do not practice ethical purchasing in a systematic way. It is also possible that at least part of this group feels that it is 'abstaining' from this politicisation of purchasing.

However, the perspective of voting is less helpful on this point. Abstaining in democratic election simply means that others get to choose who will govern next. 'Abstaining' from thinking about ethics but still making a purchase is like voting without thinking about which party is being chosen. As described in the first issue of *Ethical Consumer Magazine* in 1989:

> When we buy something without bothering to ask questions about the producer we are not 'abstaining'. The only way to abstain is to

buy nothing at all. By failing to ask these questions we can be accused of condoning or supporting practices of which we disapprove. It is the moral equivalent of entering a polling booth blindfolded – where there is a practical danger of electing the National Front [a far right party in the UK at that time].

This argument is similar to the one which says that it is not possible to discuss economic ideas in a way that does not involve politics (10.8).

It is another argument in favour of a more systematic approach to ethical purchasing. In Sections 1.6.5 and 1.6.6, we also discussed the idea that there is a responsibility to purchase ethically at every stage in the supply chain.

10.7.3 Ethical purchasing offers frequent and nuanced opportunities for additional political participation

If, as argued above, there is an essentially political or ethical element in most purchasing, it follows that each purchase is a tiny (or large in the case of a local authority road programme) opportunity to exert political influence in one direction or another. It is just as potentially flawed as ordinary democratic voting, in that it is limited by the quality of parties or products on offer.

It can also be a blunt instrument when there are multiple issues of concern: as with political parties it is rare to find one whose manifesto exactly aligns with our own views on everything. By and large, we have to go for the best available. The same is true of companies manufacturing our products.

Like electoral participation though, it works best when people are also active and campaigning and communicating between voting opportunities. In electoral politics, to solve the blunt instrument problem, people will join political parties or protest or campaign for them to take up particular issues. The same is true of ethical purchasing and, in Section 1.8 we noted how communicating the ethical nature of buying or boycott decisions to manufacturers was critical to make the whole thing work. Indeed, communication and engagement with producers, as part of collective groups or lobbies, is a running theme throughout this book and can be likened to the communication and engagement that goes on inside political parties around the detail of policy.

It should also be noted that the opportunity to exercise a purchase vote tends to occur more frequently than formal electoral opportunities. Having to wait four or five years to change a particularly annoying government can be frustrating, to say the least. And it is useful to be able to take action in markets in the interim on issues which are not receiving government support. Boycotts around South Africa during the unsympathetic Thatcher government in the UK and green purchasing during the climate change-denying years of the Trump government in the USA are just two examples.

Finally, just to reinforce the point, purchase votes are not a substitute for electoral votes. It is possible to buy a (Fairtrade) chocolate bar on the way to the polling booth, and indeed to buy a bottle of (organic) wine to celebrate victories or drown sorrows when election results are revealed.

10.7.4 It is possible that greater ethical purchaser consciousness can lead to greater organisation and use of this power

Basic principles in 1.6 stated that 'purchasers have power where there is a choice between producers'. In the same way that Marx saw that raising class consciousness among working people was essential to realising the power of organised labour, it is possible to assert that raising a similar conscious-ness among people of their power as organised ethical purchasers can lead to a greater and more effective use of this power. This applies to people as members of organisations and companies as well as people as individuals. Although this idea is not a new one, it is one of the aims of this book.

The following quote from a UK co-operative movement writer in 1920 provides an illustration of this in the florid language of that time:

> In our common everyday needs the great industries of the world take their rise. We – the mass of common men and women in all countries - also compose the world's markets. To sell to us is the ultimate aim of the world's business. Hence it is ourselves as consumers who stand in a central relation to all the economies of the world, like the king in his kingdom. As producers we go unto a particular factory, farm or mine, but as consumers we are set by nature thus to give leadership, aim and purpose to the whole economic world. That we are not kings, but serfs in the mass, is due to our failure to think and act together as consumers and so to realise our true position and power.
>
> Percy Redfern

10.8 Economics as a discipline has been slow to track, let alone theorise about the significance of ethical purchasing

10.8.1 The discipline of economics has not covered itself in glory dealing with ethical issues

Economics emerged in the 19th century as a system of thought designed to understand the new idea of self-regulating markets. As mentioned elsewhere, within capitalist economies the discipline of economics holds an exalted status for governments as many of the key collective goals for whole societies are articulated in the language of economics: GDP growth, unemployment, and inflation are, for example, three familiar words used to denote management measurements common to most governments. Within the language of traditional economics though, it is possible to observe both open hostility and disinterest towards the language of ethics.

The open hostility is epitomised in the over-quoted 1970 maxim of Milton Friedman that the only responsibility of business is to make as much money for its shareholders as possible. But it does also hark back to the 'invisible hand' of Adam Smith, the founder of modern economics, who argued that people pursuing self-interest in free markets would inadvertently improve the lot of everyone. Much has been written elsewhere, and indeed by Smith himself, unpicking many of the errors in these simplistic assumptions.

Regarding disinterest, this tends to take the view that ethics like politics belongs in a different discipline. As discussed in Section 10.1, under 'externalities' there are certain areas where even mainstream economists concede that governments need to intervene to prevent harms becoming damaging. However, many economists do not usually then discuss what these interventions should be. As with economic inequality, it is as if some economists just want to throw the subject over the fence for someone else to deal with! The paucity of enquiry to date into ethical purchasing and investment particularly within economics is therefore just one example of many of this apparent disinterest.

Mainstream economics also has a problem with ethical purchasing particularly. It classically views consumers making choices as 'acting rationally' to 'maximise their utility' – seeking the highest personal satisfaction for the lowest price. Later, ideas within behavioural economics introduced the idea of irrational consumers and the need to nudge them from time to time. The many millions of people and organisations we have met in this book purchasing with ethical considerations in mind therefore tend to be viewed by economists as anomalous, marginal, or 'niche', since they do not fit comfortably into the classical or indeed irrational definitions.

There is a long history of influential scholarly critique of the inability of mainstream economics to understand its place in a wider ethical framework. The growth of interest among European governments in measuring alternative economic indicators as well as economic growth is just one example of this. There have also been 'revolts' of students calling for a more relevant discipline, such as a group in Manchester which emerged after the banking crash of 2008. Ethical purchasing is just another specific element of this wider critique which seeks to address those elements of economic debate which fail to take ethical issues seriously.

So, although markets can change quickly when under pressure from ethical campaigners, it seems that economics, as a field of study, is falling a long way behind. There are many specific areas that appear worthy of more attention. Ethical purchasing itself is just one of them, and the beginning of a serious study into it is one of the purposes of this book. Two others (in 10.8.2 and 10.8.3) are worth mentioning, because they take the existence of ethical purchasing as a given and ask what these new markets might be able to do next in order to better address the issues that people face.

10.8.2 Can competition in markets drive up ethical standards?

Earlier on in this book, some examples of companies appearing to be acting competitively around ethical issues have been discussed. These included UK supermarkets (3.8), multiple accreditations in the coffee market (9.7), and the existence of 'mature ethical markets' generally where ethical issues had been a factor for some companies for some time (1.3.4). Indeed, any company using ethical issues in its marketing (see Chapter 9) might be said to be at least trying to act competitively on its ethics.

Another key general theme in this book is that the main cause of ethical issues appearing in markets is deliberate actions by civil society groups to engage consumers and purchasers in their cause (Chapter 3). However, once an issue is there and consumers have become aware of it and companies have begun to engage with it, there are signs that some companies may begin to compete on the way they have chosen to deal with it (3.8).

This raises the possibility of a virtuous circle whereby campaigners can move onto a different issue and companies can gradually lift standards by trying to outdo each other on ethics. If companies are talking about this publicly, they are also keeping the issue in the public mind and performing an educational role too (9.6). Of course, we know buyers are generally very price sensitive, and this will limit the impact that can be made here, but it is nonetheless an area that is under-researched and poorly understood.

Perhaps it was this idea of a self-correcting market correcting ethical abuses that Cesar Chavez was thinking of when he described his successful boycott campaign as 'capitalism in reverse' (see 10.2.5).

10.8.3 The notion of 'ethical growth' appears under-researched and theorised

The problem of making economic growth a sole target for societies in a world of finite resources has long been a problem for critics of the current economic model. With other targets like well-being increasingly being discussed and physical boundaries of the planet being non-negotiable, it is only a matter of time before new goals become increasingly important.

There is also research into the idea that it is possible to 'decouple' growth from resource use. This notion is controversial, not least because it appears to be trying to placate the very capital markets which lie at the heart of the problem in the first place.

Nevertheless, in an economic model which admits to the existence of ethical transactions, it appears that a market with a growing share for ethical products (which are slightly more expensive) could be larger than one without ethical products – since the measurement of growth is just for the value of all transactions. In Chapter 1 (1.5), an example was used of an organic bakery taking increasing market share. If one were to move into a town with only one other (non-organic) bakery and 50% of people switched to the organic option, then the value of the economy in that town will have increased by the difference in price – if all other things were to remain equal.

In a sense, this discourse is much like others around the notion of adding value to a product. The ethical history of a product can be seen as just another element which consumers may value and by making the product more 'ethical' a producer is adding value. If people will pay (a little) more for this added value across most products and services, then the scope for ethical economic growth appears significant.

Of course, if you can measure growth of non-financial factors, such as natural capital or the absence of hunger, then moving these in the right direction could be considered to be ethical growth of some kind too.

Although it is beginning, much research and thinking remains to be done is this new area.

10.9 The growth of ethical purchasing is also a key factor in the emergence of new mission-oriented company types

Charities in the UK have been trading arms since the 1960s, and even older historical examples exist of manufacturers with social as well as financial goals. Robert Owen, a founding father of the UK co-operative movement, for example, was a factory owner with model provisions for workers. However, there is little doubt that the 21st century has seen an explosion of innovation around the idea that trading companies should be able to pursue goals in addition to financial profit.

Although this is a book length subject on its own, there are four main elements to identify here and to note their relationship to the ethical purchasing movement:

(a) *Co-operatives*

Co-operatives are organisations whose goal is to serve their members interests rather than the interests of investors. They may be customer owned or worker owned, and has been operating since the 1850s to address some of the problems that business short-sightedness can create for ordinary people. As a movement, co-operatives have always been interested in serving the wider interests of society, and the rise of ethical purchasing has given many of them the confidence to embrace the supply side with gusto (see Section 9). In the UK, Switzerland, Italy, and Finland (to name but four), co-operative retailers have been at the forefront of giving the Fairtrade movement access to mass markets.

(b) *Social enterprises*

These are trading organisations set up with an overt social mission and can include charities and other non-profit company types. This is a very broad category (which sometimes crosses over with the other categories). They might provide affordable childcare in Worcester or import organic cotton T-shirts into Europe. There has been a lot of growth of these types of enterprise in the first two decades of the 21st century to supply both ethical consumers and other buyers like local authorities interested in supporting this approach to business (see Section 5.2.4).

(c)   *B-corporations*

B-corporations are a relatively recent US invention which retains profit distribution to shareholders but formally embeds social mission into the governing documents of the organisation. It has grown very quickly since then and now boasts over 4,000 registered B-corporations around the world. It is relatively easy for ordinary businesses to convert into this company type and some well-known consumer brands like Patagonia (clothing) and Ben & Jerry's (ice cream) have joined up. The B-corporation movement explicitly refers to the rise of ethical interest amongst consumers as critical to its development.

(d)   *Brand activism*

There is increasing interest in the idea that consumer brands can behave like NGOs or Civil society organisations in consumer markets addressing pressing political issues of the day. Body Shop was one of the earliest examples of this kind of approach (see 4.3.3), but increasingly mainstream brands are becoming involved. One example from 2018 was Nike's use of anti-racist American footballer Colin Kaepernick in its adverts in direct opposition to the US president's language and comments around this issue. All company types can be brand activists. Sometimes, but not always, brand activism can be designed to draw attention to ethical products (Body Shop campaigned around Fairtrade Brazil Nuts from the Amazon for example). The idea that there is a broader trend towards a merging of roles between campaigners and traders was discussed in an academic work on the ethical consumer in 2005.

10.9.1 There is also an emergence of ethical labels or certifications for mission-oriented business

Although any company can convert into one with B-corporation type rules, there is also a voluntary B-corporation certification scheme on top of this to further convince purchasers that the move is genuine. It was set up by the non-profit group B Lab in Pennsylvania in 2006 and scores a company across five areas: Environment, Workers, Customers, Community, and Governance.

These standards are holistic, are based around already established third party benchmarks where possible, and operate at a company rather than a product level. In addition, B Lab licences on-product logos for corporations meeting the standards and recognises the importance of bringing consumers along as part of the movement.

The UK has a similar home-grown version of the same thing called the Social Enterprise Mark. Its accreditations tend to be found on less obviously commercial operations like universities and healthcare providers.

Although not as sophisticated as the B-Corp or Social Enterprise Mark accreditations, the co-operative movement introduced its own 'co-op' logo internationally in 2013 to help people identify genuine co-operative businesses too.

10.9.2 This movement towards certifying whole companies rather than products can address other issues such as product label narrowness

As we saw in Section 8.4.3, one of the criticisms of some ethical certification schemes was that by certifying just one aspect of production, they could mislead people to think that other areas were problem-free too. Although the B-Corps certification is quite generous to companies, it does at least address the issue of narrowness.

In addition, some schemes have been criticised because they have certified one subsidiary of a company which is meeting high standards whilst other parts of the company are continuing to carry out damaging activities. Greenpeace's 2018 report 'The Final Countdown' identified that this was occurring with RSPO certification and 23 palm oil plantation companies in Indonesia, including Austindo Nusantera Jaya and the Bumitima group.

Of course, not all company-level certifications address the issue of label narrowness. The Fair Tax Mark, for example, which certifies that no tax avoidance activities are taking place, has to operate a company group level to make sense. While it is narrow in this respect, it is interesting to reflect how companies certified under this scheme tend to stand out as ethical in other respects too.

References and notes

10.1.1 Stephen Mundy (2000) Markets and Market Failure, Heinemann – Studies in Economics and Business.

10.1.3 William Greider (1992) *Who Will Tell the People: The Betrayal of America Democracy.* Simon and Schuster. New York.

George Monbiot (2000) *Captive State: The Corporate Takeover of Britain.* Pan Books. London.

BBC News Website (11/12/18) Trump rolls back decades of Clean Water Act protections; https://www.bbc.co.uk/news/world-us-canada-46526776

Lobbying and antibiotics; see e.g. L. H. Kahn (2016) *One Health and the Politics of Antimicrobial Resistance.* John Hopkins University Press. Baltimore.

10.1.4 The Levin Institute – The State University of New York (2016); www.globalization101.org/the-tuna-dolphin-case/

The Atlantic (Jan 6, 2014) The Dark Side of Globalization: Why Seattle's 1999 Protesters Were Right; www.theatlantic.com/business/archive/2014/01/the-dark-side-of-globalization-why-seattles-1999-protesters-were-right/282831/

See e.g. World Trade Organisation (August 2020) Environmental requirements and market access: Preventing 'green protectionism'; www.wto.org/english/tratop_e/envir_e/envir_req_e.htm

Global Justice Now (August 2020) What is TTIP?; www.globaljustice.org.uk/what-ttip-0

10.1.4 (a) See e.g. Chan, Anita (2003) A "race to the bottom": Globalisation and China's labour standards. *Third World Quarterly,* 24(6), pp. 1011–1028.

Barnet and Muller (1976) Global Reach: The Power of the Multinational Corporations

(b) OECD (2013) Action Plan on Base Erosion and Profit Shifting, OECD Publishing; http://dx.doi.org/10.1787/9789264202719-en

10.1.5 Stern Review on the Economics of Climate Change (2006) For the UK government.

For lobbying's role in COP, see e.g. www.theguardian.com/environment/2015/nov/26/paris-climate-change-conference-circus-comes-to-town

10.2.2 The grouping together of certified producers into a lobby for intervention was discussed in more detail in 3.1.1.

10.2.3 For shaming of corporations to join the Bangladesh Fire and Safety Accord, see e.g www.ethicalconsumer.org/fashion-clothing/rana-plaza-five-years Fairtrade Foundation (2019) Competition Law and Sustainability; www.fairtrade.org.uk/wp-content/uploads/legacy/doc/Competition%20Law%20and%20Sustainability%20-%20Fairtrade%20Report.pdf

10.2.4 N. Craig Smith (1990) *Morality and the Market*. Routledge. London is good on Cesar Chavez and the grape boycott, and is where most of this detail is referenced.

10.3.1 K. Carstens (1967) Apartheid, Church and politics: The response of the Church in the USA to apartheid. *Africa Today*, 14(1), *Africa in American Politics* (1967), pp. 19–22. Indiana University Press. For Vietnam War connection, see e.g. Brian Hicks (2014) PaxWorld Continues to Up the Ante; https://www.greenchipstocks.com/articles/socially-responsible-investing-paxworld-investments/80040

Stats on the scale of ethical investment are from the 2018 Global Sustainable Investment Review from the Global Sustainable Investment Alliance; http://www.gsi-alliance.org/wp-content/uploads/2019/03/GSIR_Review2018.3.28.pdf

Some good ethical investment books include: T. Hebb et al. (eds) (2019) *The Routledge Handbook of Responsible Investment*. Abingdon. R. Sparkes (2010) *Socially Responsible Investment: A Global Revolution*. Wiley. New Jersey. A. Lewis (2002) *Morals, Markets and Money: The Case of Ethical Investing*. Financial Times Series. Financial Times Prentice Hall. Harlow.

10.3.2 Much has been written on the China 2008 Melamine Scandal, including www.theguardian.com/world/2009/nov/24/china-executes-milk-scandal-pair

The lobbying campaign against traffic light labelling in food has been well covered in *Ethical Consumer Magazine*, including in ECXX September/October 2007 at p 22. The same is true of the Stop Funding Hate campaign in the UK. See e.g. the February 2018 article at www.ethicalconsumer.org/ethicalcampaigns/stop-funding-hate

The Times, 8 November 2019; https://www.thetimes.co.uk/article/ppi-claims-take-co-operative-bank-losses-to-118-6m-brrrjgfhq

10.3.3 *The Guardian*; www.theguardian.com/commentisfree/2016/jul/13/the-problem-with-selling-a-lethal-product-you-just-cant-get-the-staff

10.4.2 Human Rights Watch (2019) US: States Use Anti-Boycott Laws to Punish Responsible Businesses; https://www.hrw.org/news/2019/04/23/us-states-use-anti-boycott-laws-punish-responsible-businesses

France 24 (2016) France's criminalisation of Israel boycotts sparks free speech debate; www.france24.com/en/20160120-france-boycott-israel-bds-law-free-speech-antisemitism

10.4.3 See e.g. Lynn Stout (2012) *The Shareholder Value Myth: How Putting Shareholders First Harms Investors, Corporations, and the Public.* Berrell-Koehler.

For B Corporation, see Andrew Kassoy, Bart Houlahan and Jay Coen Gilbet (2016) Impact governance and management: Fulfilling the promise of capitalism to achieve a shared and durable prosperity. Brookings Institute July 2016, where B Lab founders are quoted as saying: "A marketplace lacking common impact metrics and credible data prevents consumers, workers, companies, investors, policymakers, and other stakeholders from rewarding those companies that can demonstrate that they are creating a material positive impact on society."

10.5.1 M. Sandel (2020) The Tyranny of Merit is one of many books to talk about the role of economics narrowing ethical discourse.

10.5.3 Clive Barnett, Paul Cloke, Nick Clarke and Alice Malpass (2011) *Globalizing Responsibility: The Political Rationalities of Ethical Consumption.* RGS-IBG Book Series. Wiley-Blackwell. Oxford.

10.5.4 Michelle Micheletti (2003) *Political Virtue and Shopping: Individuals, Consumerism, and Collective Action.* Palgrave Macmillan.

www.reuters.com (10/5/19) Muslims afraid, resentful as ethnic divide deepens in Sri Lanka

By A. Ananthalakshmi, Ranga Sirilal; www.reuters.com/article/us-sri-lanka-blasts-backlash-idUSKCN1SG0TU

www.bbc.co.uk (25/3/13) The hardline Buddhists targeting Sri Lanka's Muslims; https://www.bbc.co.uk/news/world-asia-21840600

For discourses around cultural appropriation, see e.g. Rachel Kuo (2016) How Cultural Appropriation Becomes Trendy – And the Real Cost of Our Consumerism; https://everydayfeminism.com/2016/09/cultural-appropriation-trends/; and

Crane, W (2018) Cultural formation and appropriation in the era of merchant capitalism. *Historical Materialism*, 26(2), pp. 242–270.

Blue-washing is a technique employed by corporates and companies to form collaborations and associations with various UN Agencies; https://sarvahitey.wordpress.com/2018/05/16/greenwashing-and-blue-washing/

10.6.1 UNEP (2005) Protecting the ozone layer Vol 5A: aerosols, sterilants, carbon tetrachloride. and miscellaneous uses; https://

wedocs.unep.org/bitstream/handle/20.500.11822/29497/Ozone.
pdf?sequence=1&isAllowed=y

10.6.2.   Captain Boycott is widely discussed and also here: N. Craig Smith
(1990) Morality and the Market. Routledge. London.

Boycotts of stores in South Africa. Purchasing Power – Civil Action for
Sustainable Consumption (1998) Zadek, Lingayah and Murphy: NEF UK.

10.6.3 Confronting the Crisis of Global Governance: June 2015. The Report of
the Commission on Global Security, Justice, and Governance; www.
stimson.org/wp-content/files/file-attachments/Commission_on_
Global_Security_Justice%20_Governance_0.pdf

For competition policy, see World Economic Forum (Dec 2019) White
Paper: Competition Policy in a Globalized, Digitalized Economy.

10.7.1 N. Craig Smith (cited in 10.6.2 and widely elsewhere) is amongst
those arguing that ethical purchasing is an argument in favour of
capitalism.

See also R. Dickinson and M. Carsky (2005) The consumer as
economic voter, in *The Ethical Consumer*, Edited by Harrison, Newholm
and Shaw. Sage. London.

10.7.2 *Ethical Consumer Magazine* (March 1989) Issue 1. Ethics and the
Consumer p. 6.

10.7.4 Percy Redfern (1920) The Consumers' Place In Society.

10.8.1 Whole libraries of literature have been generated on the subject of this
paragraph from Marx onwards. A specifically ethical or more often an
ecological economics has been a subject of focus since at least the 1970s.
Prominent theorists at that time appeared in Daly, Herman E. (1973)
Economics, Ecology, Ethics. Essays towards a steady-state economy.
And later in Herman E. Daly, John B. Cobb, Jr (1989) For the common
good: Redirecting the economy toward community, the environment,
and a sustainable future.

Milton Friedman (1970) The social responsibility of business is to
increase its profits. *The New York Times Magazine*, September 13.

Looking for the ethics in Adam Smith's work on economics is a
popular sport for many. See e.g. Cristovam Buarque (1993) *The End of
Economics or Wells*, Thomas (2014) Recovering Adam Smith's ethical
economics real-world economics review, issue no. 68

Richard H. Thaler and Cass R. Sunstein (2008). *Nudge: Improving
Decisions about Health, Wealth, and Happiness*. Yale University Press.
New Haven.

B. Bleys (2012) Beyond GDP: Classifying alternative measures for progress. *Social Indicator Research*, 109, pp. 355–376; https://doi.org/10.1007/s11205-011-9906-6

www.theguardian.com/education/2013/nov/18/academics-back-student-protests-neoclassical-economics-teaching

10.8.3 Kate Raworth (2017) *Doughnut Economics*. Random House. London.

James Ward et al. (2017) The decoupling delusion: Rethinking growth and sustainability; https://theconversation.com/the-decoupling-delusion-rethinking-growth-and-sustainability-71996

10.9 P. Develtere and I. Pollet (2005) Co-operatives and Fair Trade; http://www.aciamericas.coop/IMG/pdf/Cooperatives-and-fair-trade.pdf

Urdal David (2011) *Beyond the Corporation: Humanity Working*. Bodeley Head. London.

Liam Kay (2018) Social enterprises 'contribute £6obn to the economy each year'; www.thirdsector.co.uk/social-enterprises-contribute-6obn-economy-year/social-enterprise/article/1493336

On B Corporations, see e.g. Bart Houlahan, Andrew Kassoy and Jay Coen Gilbert (2016) Impact governance and management: Fulfilling the promise of capitalism to achieve a shared and durable prosperity; www.brookings.edu/research/impact-governance-and-management-fulfilling-the-promise-of-capitalism-to-achieve-a-shared-and-durable-prosperity/

Christian Sarkar and Philip Kotler (2018) Brand activism: From purpose to action.

Jill Avery and Koen Pauwels (2020) Brand Activism: Nike and Colin Kaepernick. Harvard Business School Teaching Note 520-104, May 2020 (Revised July 2020).

Pressure Groups, Campaigns and Consumers in Harrison, Newholm and Shaw (2005) *The Ethical Consumer*. Sage. London.

10.9.1 https://bcorporation.net/certification, www.socialenterprisemark.org.uk, www.theguardian.com/social-enterprise-network/2013/nov/04/coop-international-marque-launched

10.9.2 Greenpeace Report (2018) The final countdown: Now or never to reform the palm oil industry;

https://fairtaxmark.net/accredited-organisations/

Appendix 1

SOME BROAD ETHICAL FRAMEWORKS IN USE TODAY

Section 1.1.3 looked at areas of ethics where it could be said that there were some consensual values. It went on to say that some philosophers have suggested that globalisation has brought with it some emerging global ethical values.

This appendix contains details from five broad ethical frameworks.

The first is the UN's 17 Sustainable Development goals.

Two are reporting frameworks for large corporations. One comes from the French Government and one, the GRI, from a multi-stakeholder project involving companies too.

Two come from campaign groups or civil society. One from the giant collective project the Business Human Rights Benchmark and one from the tiny UK CSO Ethical Consumer.

They also appear here as an illustration of how language and discourse around production in the 21st century is not all about profit and economic efficiency (see also 10.5).

Table A1   UN Sustainable Development Goals – Set by the UN General Assembly in 2015

		Human rights
Goal 1	No poverty	End poverty in all its forms everywhere.
Goal 2	Zero hunger	End hunger, achieve food security and improved nutrition, and promote sustainable agriculture.
Goal 3	Good health and well-being for people	Ensure healthy lives and promote well-being for all at all ages.
Goal 4	Quality education	Ensure inclusive and equitable quality education and promote lifelong learning opportunities for all.
Goal 5	Gender equality	Achieve gender equality and empower all women and girls.
Goal 6	Clean water and sanitation	Ensure availability and sustainable management of water and sanitation for all.
Goal 7	Affordable and clean energy	Ensure access to affordable, reliable, sustainable, and modern energy for all.
Goal 8	Decent work and economic growth	Promote sustained, inclusive, and sustainable economic growth, full and productive employment, and decent work for all.
		Environmental
Goal 11	Sustainable cities and communities	Make cities and human settlements inclusive, safe, resilient, and sustainable.
Goal 13	Climate action	Take urgent action to combat climate change and its impacts by regulating emissions and promoting developments in renewable energy.
Goal 14	Life below water	Conserve and sustainably use the oceans, seas, and marine resources for sustainable development.
Goal 15	Life on land	Protect, restore, and promote sustainable use of terrestrial ecosystems, sustainably manage forests, combat desertification, and halt and reverse land degradation and halt biodiversity loss.
		Technical
Goal 9	Industry, innovation, and infrastructure	Build resilient infrastructure, promote inclusive and sustainable industrialization, and foster innovation.
Goal 10	Reducing inequalities	Reduce income inequality within and among countries.
Goal 12	Responsible consumption and production	Ensure sustainable consumption and production patterns.
Goal 16	Peace, justice, and strong institutions	Promote peaceful and inclusive societies for sustainable development, provide access to justice for all, and build effective, accountable, and inclusive institutions at all levels.
Goal 17	Partnerships for the goals	Strengthen the means of implementation and revitalize the global partnership for sustainable development.

(Author's categorisation by Human Rights, Environmental, and Technical).

Table A2 Categories for Mandatory Social and Environmental Reporting in France (see 6.6.1 b)

Social indicators	(a) Employment	The total workforce and workforce broken down by gender, age, and religion
		Hiring of employees and redundancies
		Compensation and its evolution
	(b) Work organisation	Working hours
		Absenteeism
	(c) Labour relations	Organization of social dialogue
		Outcome of the collective agreements
	(d) Health and safety	Health and safety conditions at work
		Outcome of the collective agreements signed with trade unions regarding occupational health and safety
		Frequency and seriousness of incident and occupational diseases
	(e) Training policies	Total training hours
	(f) Equal treatment	Policies and measures promoting gender equality
		Policies and measures taken to promote the employment and integration of disabled persons
		Policies and actions taken to prevent discrimination
	(g) Promotion and enforcement of the ILO's basic conventions	Respecting freedom of association and collective bargaining
		Elimination of discrimination in employment and occupation
		Elimination of forced or compulsory labour
Environmental indicators	(a) General environmental policy	Company efforts to take into account environmental issues and, where appropriate, assessments or environmental certifications
		Employee training programmes on environmental protection
		Resources devoted to prevention of environmental risks and pollution
		Financial provisions for environmental risks
	(b) Pollution and waste management	Measures to prevent, reduce, or compensate for air, water, and soil emissions severely affecting the environment
		Measures to prevent, recycle, and dispose of waste

(Continued)

		Taking into account noise and other forms of pollution
	(c) Sustainable use of resources	Water use and water supply based on local constraints
		The consumption of raw materials and measures taken to improve their efficiency
		Energy consumption, measures to improve energy efficiency, and percentage of renewable energy used
		Land use
	(d) Climate change	Greenhouse gas emissions
		Adaptation to climate change impacts
	(e) Protection of biodiversity	Measures taken to preserve or enhance biodiversity
Societal indicators	(a) Impact of the company's territorial, economic, and social activity	Employment and regional development
		Neighbouring and local populations
	(b) External relations with individuals or organisations interested in the company's activities	Opportunities for dialogue with these individuals or organisations
		Corporate philanthropy
	(c) Subcontracting and suppliers	Taking into account social and environmental issues in purchasing policies
		Importance of subcontracting and integration of CSR in the relationships with suppliers and subcontractors
	(d) Fair operating practices	Actions implemented to prevent any kind of corruption
		Measures implemented to promote consumer health and safety
	(e) Human rights	Other actions promoting human rights

Table A3 Ethical Consumer Magazine Ranking Categories for
           Corporations June 2019

Environment	Sustainability reporting
	Climate change
	Pollution and toxics
	Habitats and resources
	Palm oil
Animals	Animal testing
	Factory farming
	Animal rights
People	Human rights
	Workers' rights
	Supply chain workers' rights
	Human health
	Armaments
Company ethos	Tax conduct
	Directors' pay
	Business lobbying
	Controversial technologies
	Radical governance (positive)
	(Boycott Call)

Table A4 Headings from Corporate Human Rights Benchmark Methodology 2019 for the
           Agricultural Products, Apparel, and Extractives Industries

Governance and policy commitments

A.1 Policy commitments

A.1.1 Commitment to respect human rights

A.1.2 Commitment to respect the human rights of workers

A.1.3 Commitment to respect human rights particularly relevant to the industry

A.1.3.a Land and natural resources – Agricultural products industry

A.1.3.b People's rights – Agricultural products industry

A.1.3 Apparel industry

A.1.3 Extractives industry

A.1.4 Commitment to engage with stakeholders

A.1.5 Commitment to remedy

A.1.6 Commitment to respect the rights of human rights defenders

A.2 Board level accountability

A.2.1 Commitment from the top

A.2.2 Board discussions

A.2.3 Incentives and performance management

C. Grievance mechanisms

C.1 Grievance channels/mechanisms to receive complaints or concerns from workers

C.2 Grievance channels/mechanisms to receive complaints or concerns from external individuals and communities

C.3 Users are involved in the design and performance of the channel(s)/mechanism(s)

C.4 Procedures related to the mechanism(s)/channel(s) are publicly available and explained

C.5 Commitment to non-retaliation over concerns/complaints made

C.6 Company involvement with State-based judicial and non-judicial grievance mechanisms

C.7 Remedying adverse impacts and incorporating lessons learned

(*Continued*)

Embedding respect and human rights due diligence

B.1 Embedding respect for human rights in company culture and management systems
B.1.1 Responsibility and resources for day-to-day human rights functions
B.1.2 Incentives and performance management
B.1.3 Integration with enterprise risk management
B.1.4 Communication/dissemination of policy commitment(s)
B.1.4.a Communication/dissemination of policy commitment(s) within company's own operations
B.1.4.b Communication/dissemination of policy commitment(s) to business relationships
B.1.5 Training on human rights
B.1.6 Monitoring and corrective actions
B.1.7 Engaging business relationships
B.1.8 Approach to engagement with potentially affected stakeholders
B.2 Human rights due diligence
B.2.1 Identifying: Processes and triggers for identifying human rights risks and impacts
B.2.2 Assessing: Assessment of risks and impacts identified (salient risks and key industry risks)
B.2.3 Integrating and acting: Integrating assessment findings internally and taking appropriate action
B.2.4 Tracking: Monitoring and evaluating the effectiveness of actions to respond to human rights risks and impacts
B.2.5 Communicating: Accounting for how human rights impacts are addressed

D.1 Agricultural products
D.1.1 Living wage
D.1.1.a Living wage (in own agricultural operations)
D.1.1.b Living wage (in the supply chain)
D.1.2 Aligning purchasing decisions with human rights
D.1.3 Mapping and disclosing the supply chain
D.1.4 Prohibition on child labour
D.1.4.a Age verification and corrective actions (in own agricultural operations)
D.1.4.b Age verification and corrective actions (in the supply chain)
D.1.5 Prohibition on forced labour
D.1.5.a Debt bondage and other unacceptable financial costs (in own agricultural operations)
D.1.5.b Debt bondage and other unacceptable financial costs (in the supply chain)
D.1.5.c Restrictions on workers (in own agricultural operations)
D.1.5.d Restrictions on workers (in the supply chain)
D.1.6 Freedom of association and collective bargaining
D.1.6.a Freedom of association and collective bargaining (in own agricultural operations)
D.1.6.b Freedom of association and collective bargaining (in the supply chain)
D.1.7 Health and safety
D.1.7.a Fatalities, lost days, injury rates (in own agricultural operations)
D.1.7.b Fatalities, lost days, injury rates (in the supply chain)
D.1.8 Land rights
D.1.8.a Land acquisition (in own agricultural operations)
D.1.8.b Land acquisition (in the supply chain)
D.1.9 Water and sanitation
D.1.9.a Water and sanitation (in own agricultural operations)
D.1.9.b Water and sanitation (in the supply chain)
D.1.10 Women's rights
D.1.10.a Women's rights (in own agricultural operations)
D.1.10.b Women's rights (in the supply chain)

Table A5 Index of Consolidated Set of GRI Sustainability Reporting Standards 2018

Universal standards
GRI 101: *Foundation 2016* (containing Standard Interpretation 1)
GRI 102: *General Disclosures 2016*
GRI 103: *Management Approach 2016* (1 July 2018)

Topic-specific standards
GRI 200: Economic
GRI 201: *Economic Performance 2016*
GRI 202: *Market Presence 2016*
GRI 203: *Indirect Economic Impacts 2016*
GRI 204: *Procurement Practices 2016*
GRI 205: *Anti-corruption 2016*
GRI 206: *Anti-competitive Behaviour 2016*
GRI 300: Environmental
GRI 301: *Materials 2016*
GRI 302: *Energy 2016*
GRI 303: *Water and Effluents 2018*
GRI 304: *Biodiversity 2016*
GRI 305: *Emissions 2016*
GRI 306: *Effluents and Waste 2016*
GRI 307: *Environmental Compliance 2016*
GRI 308: *Supplier Environmental Assessment 2016*
GRI 400: Social
GRI 401: *Employment 2016* (containing Standard Interpretation 1)
GRI 402: *Labor/Management Relations 2016*
GRI 403: *Occupational Health and Safety 2018*
GRI 404: *Training and Education 2016*
GRI 405: *Diversity and Equal Opportunity 2016*
GRI 406: *Non-Discrimination 2016*
GRI 407: *Freedom of Association and Collective Bargaining 2016*
GRI 408: *Child Labor 2016*
GRI 409: *Forced or Compulsory Labor 2016*
GRI 410: *Security Practices 2016*
GRI 411: *Rights of Indigenous Peoples 2016*
GRI 412: *Human Rights Assessment 2016*
GRI 413: *Local Communities 2016*
GRI 414: *Supplier Social Assessment 2016*
GRI 415: *Public Policy 2016*
GRI 416: *Customer Health and Safety 2016*
GRI 417: *Marketing and Labelling 2016*
GRI 418: *Customer Privacy 2016*
GRI 419: *Socio-Economic Compliance 2016* (1 July 2018)

INDEX